NAKED AND ERECT

Other books by Joel Ryce-Menuhin

The Self in Early Childhood
Jungian Sandplay: The Wonderful Therapy
Jung and the Monotheisms: Judaism, Christianity and Islam (Editor)

NAKED AND ERECT

Male Sexuality and Feeling

JOEL RYCE-MENUHIN

CHIRON PUBLICATIONS • WILMETTE, ILLINOIS

Permissions

The Collected Works of C. G. Jung. Copyright © by Routledge & Kegan Paul. Excerpts, cited passim, are reprinted by permission of Routledge.

The Self in Early Childhood by Joel Ryce-Menuhin. Copyright © 1988 by Free Association Books. Excerpts reprinted by permission of Free Association Books.

"Some Plain Talk About Men" by Joel Ryce-Menuhin appeared in *Harvest* 35, 1989–90, Journal for Jungian Studies, Analytical Psychology Club London. Copyright © 1989 by Joel Ryce-Menuhin. Excerpts, cited passim, were adapted by permission.

Library of Congress Catalog Card Number: 96-25222

Printed in the United States of America.
Copyedited by Andrew C. Baker.
Book design by Vivian Bradbury.
Cover design by D. J. Hyde.

Library of Congress Cataloging-in-Publication Data:

Ryce-Menuhin, Joel.
   Naked and erect : male sexuality and feeling / Joel Ryce-Menuhin.
      p. cm.
Includes bibliographical references and index.
ISBN 1-888602-00-7 (pbk.)
   1. Masculinity (Psychology) 2. Men—Psychology. 3. Sex (Psychology)
4. Jungian psychology. I. Title.
BF175.5.M37R93 1996
155.3¢32—dc20   96-25222
                                                 CIP

ISBN 1-888602-00-7

Dedicated to Saint Joseph,
custodian of Jesus Christ,
patron of all fathers and
all easement of human death.

Contents

Foreword

TO BE INCLUSIVE, to be exploratory, and to be descriptive about male sexuality—without judgment, clinical distancing, or ideological imperatives—is with the best of psychological writers something of a daunting *attempt*. Joel Ryce-Menuhin embedded this matter in his original subtitle to his work: *Essays* on Male Sexuality and Feeling [italics mine]. Masturbation, homosexuality, heterosexuality, and bisexuality suggest the domains of sexual activity; crises and loneliness suggest the domains of inner and hence psychological existence in the realm of emotions. Here, beyond categories, Ryce-Menuhin explores how a man might express all forms of sexual activity, and how groups of men represent the categories of imperative expressions. All men, one would like to think, know feelings; forms of sexual expression are charged with cathexes, excitements, and visceral necessities.

One ponders the *moralities* of male sexuality, the *mores* of male sexuality, and the *lore* of male sexuality. The power of the active imagination combines with the unbridled explorations of dream imagination to propel sexuality into autoerotic fantasies, combined partner fantasies and seekings, and the narrative imperative to tell the tales of potency. Unfortunately, there is no known force that morally can limit the imagination, though there are mores that would limit, if not punish, the expression of sexual imaginings. The lore of male sexuality, however, is preserved in the sacred and profane expressions found in art, literature, and public performance. It is not an exaggeration to observe that every male develops, expresses, and countenances individual delineations of these moralities, mores, and lore.

What Ryce-Menuhin contributes to the substantive literature on sexuality is a valorization of the range of human sexual expression. To the extent that he does so, the reader is advised with a prefatory *caveat emptor*. The reader must be one with Terence, profoundly acknowledging that "nothing that is human is alien to me." The book itself is something of a call to a wholeness and inclusiveness that men can, do, and will express in sexual enactments.

Leland H. Roloff

Leland H. Roloff, Ph.D., is a training analyst at the C. G. Jung Institute of Chicago and Emeritus Professor of Performance Studies at Northwestern University in Evanston, Illinois.

Acknowledgments

I WANT TO THANK Dr. Leland H. Roloff, the distinguished Chicago analyst, for the foreword to this book. Dr. Andrew C. Baker has been a most helpful editorial advisor for the final manuscript. To all at Chiron Publications, I extend my warm appreciation for your cooperation in creating this concrete form of my thoughts.

Thanks go to Free Association Books, London, for permission to quote at length from my book *The Self in Early Childhood* and to Routledge, London and New York, for permission for all quotations from *The Collected Works of C. G. Jung*.

Joel Ryce-Menuhin

Introduction

MEN HAVE NEVER been less well understood by women or by other men than they seem to be today. There is such a loss of contact with reality concerning the masculine I have felt fired to write this book from experience—the experience of sixty years in a male body, spirit, and mind—in the hope that other men will be stimulated to continue the search within themselves for their understanding of what being a man may partly entail. Inevitably, as a practicing Jungian analyst, I may include some analytical ideas within the experiential, theoretical, and clinical base.

As men experiment with giving greater nurturing both at home and at work, I have heard the claim that men have "breast-envy" of women. We do not. If I express warmth and affectionate brotherly love towards men, some of them fear me, or presume me to be bisexual. I have been married for thirty-six years. I believe in marriage, but only if two people like it. I also believe men should be free not to marry, as women are, if they prefer. I greatly admire some men who happen to be bisexual or homosexual as I admire certain bisexual or lesbian women where common interests or appreciation of their talents and personalities brings me closer to them. I adore children unreservedly, not because my own child was lost to a miscarriage, but because I know how to give children a great deal of nurturing (without having breasts), and I need the return of their affection. I sense and am aware of my generation, several of the former ones and the next one. I know that I will die with a great deal of work and loving and living not yet accomplished.

I know what I have been and what that being has felt like as a man. I do not know what I may become or where my personal needs may move. Neither does anyone else if

they are sincere with themselves. I hope my readers may
benefit from my frankness and my concern. That is all I can
offer my wife, my family, my friends, my patients, my readers, my audience, and my neighborly acquaintances on the
path of life. I consider men to be undervalued, underrated,
overworked usually, too modest, and often undercompen-
sated by society for what they offer it. I thus find the claims
of some women that most men seem to be chauvinist pigs a
questionable idea in view of the male behavior I observe
around me. Of course, there are some chauvinist pigs
around; some of them are men and some of them are
women.

It has been a lifelong tendency and privilege of mine to
move among all social classes. This is because I do not see
one class as inferior or superior to another but find the color
of differences and the shared interests between classes the
hope of a future society. If we have attacked the ecology of
nature, I believe the ecology of being a man needs some
tending—both by men and by women—and I hope this book
will give encouragement to those of my readers, whatever
their gender or sexual preference, who wish to move towards
a rediscovery of masculinity in its essence now that we are
approaching the year 2000, and the dreams of a future age in
which human beings might consider liking and even loving
each other. Perhaps we will learn to love ourselves.

I like being in a male body. I like male psychology and
what it may entail. I like searching for spiritual values with
my brothers and sisters. I believe it is very different to be a
man than to be a woman. I celebrate that difference; I even
praise God that it is so. I also love the sameness in my
brothers and sisters and applaud them.

To Everyman: I salute you and I want to respect you.

To Everywoman: I salute you and I want to respect you.

To Everychild: I love you because you have already been
partly destroyed by others' failure to know you.

In this plain-speaking book about masculine sexuality
and some of its feeling aspects, I hope to activate and open
up ideas about men's ongoing problems of development. The
masculine makes up one half of the given cosmos we know:
not more, but not less!

When I first started my analytic practice in London, in

1978, I was forty-five years old, having spent the first half of my life as a concert pianist. I had not anticipated the degree of intimate trust men would bring me concerning their sexual lives, neither had my training prepared me for this. It was very moving to meet this need in my male analysands with every bit of experience and study I could muster. As time passed, I found more and more that sexual theories did very little to help these men in their actual situations. It was rather the talking cure that happened and helped. Existentially these men patients wanted reassurance that their particular version of sexuality could be discussed, analyzed, accepted, and sometimes changed, if that is what they came to want. Men have tended to keep their sexual frustrations and unhappiness away from a generalized or public media attack on women. Women have, on the contrary, splashed their sexual unhappiness across the media, hitting out constantly at men's sexual behavior as being at fault.

In these essays or chapters, which were originally developed both for public lectures and teaching seminars, I have tried to be simple, straightforward, and honest in the material cited in order to keep the whole instinctual level of sexuality present within the written word. I gained the courage to publish this material from therapy trainees, medical doctors, analysands, colleagues, and large conference audiences who encouraged this project. One night at a clinical seminar, a man whom I did not know said in the discussion period, "I have waited all my life to meet you and to hear someone speak about sex the way you do."

With that remark I felt called to put this book together, in the hope that others as well might be helped in some way by its publication. Where my work is original, that will reveal itself. Where I quote others, I have chosen those authorities whose work feels most legitimate and useful to blend in with my approach. In this volume I have aimed my discussion at masturbation, homosexuality, heterosexuality, bisexuality, and middle- and later-life experiences, as these concern male feeling-toned complexes.

For Jung, a man's greatest sexual achievement was separation from mother, with mother as a negative or positive aspect in real life as well as mother as a symbol of the unconscious. As long as a man remains dependent upon the unconscious, his libido—not as desire or as energy, but as psychological purpose—prevents his ego from directing the self. In interpreting the hero myth as sexual, a mistake is made because the blocks to happy and fulfilled sexual union for a man do not come about so much from without as from within. Men torture themselves and fight about their own sexuality from within; if the libido sinks into its own depths, introversion brings forward the darkest memories back to the source from which life first flowed—the navel connected umbilically to mother. This tie may annihilate the infant, or it can be the connection to new life.

After a man's libido plunges into this underworld it discovers a renewed fountain of youth. Through regression, the libido picks up unconscious contents that were latent. Sexual regression occurs when new libido orientations and adaptations are necessary; emergent archetypal images express libido's need of the moment. As the unconscious is greater than mother, who only symbolizes the further reaches of the life force, one has to first conquer the fear of incest in order to gain possession of the treasure hard to attain; this treasure is marvelously satisfying orgasms within the body of the partner.

Sons are notoriously unconscious of their own incestuous tendencies and project them onto the mother. If the instinctive forces of the unconscious are disregarded, they break through in opposition. A son's forward-moving libido, as conscious, demands separation from other; yet his childish longing for mother maintains a psychic resistance to separating (whether she is positive or negative to the son) which leads to neurotic fears and blocks an adaptation toward reality, toward basic common sense and balanced observation. Without these, a man's path is beset with panic; the inner man gets cut off from general life, as it is progressing, by the mother-imago.

Success in a man's life also cuts him off from his unconscious. Gilgamesh is a case in point. Jung writes, "he was so successful that the gods, the representatives of the unconscious, saw themselves compelled to deliberate how they could best bring about his downfall. Their efforts were unavailing at first, but when the hero had won the herb of immortality and was almost at his goal, a serpent stole the elixir of life from him while he slept" (Jung 1952, par. 457).

Here the serpent appears to rob Gilgamesh of energy, including sexual libido, but in fact the snake symbolizes a man's unconscious whose "alien tendencies are beginning to check the forward striving of the conscious mind" (Jung 1952, par. 458). When men do separate from mother, it is heroic but short-lived—for in the second half of life the assimilation of the contrasexual libido becomes important for the mother-symbol which no longer regresses one to the infantile acting out of the earlier male stages, but begins to point toward a creative matrix of the future. The ego and the unconscious begin further relativization in which entry into the mother is positive. As more of the Self becomes known to the ego in the second half of life, the heavy burden of the male as hero is usually a cross to carry of some sort (the cross being his wholeness as both God and animal). This becomes a psychological awareness and causes men to begin to reach beyond sexuality and to move towards divine impulses, glimpses, and desires. The tremendous tension of opposites, held in the older man as paradoxically a oneness, consumes much psychic energy that earlier was at the disposal of sexual impulse more entirely. In other words, once the hero delivers himself from the mother archetype (that is, from the infantile unconsciousness of the male's bondage to mother's authority, as is represented in the conscious ego), he then must encounter and assimilate further the anima, as lifelong partner, in gaining more insightful perspectives to his own complex fate caught up within his unique complexities.

Jung's central discovery in masculine psychology was the anima. In men, it is a nonerotic, spiritual, feminine archetype that projects onto women in its ego-images. It is related to sex most obviously in the choice of a feminine partner and it leads away from male, heroic self-mastery towards an empathic life participation. Experiencing anima is an initiatory experience—a painful submission to an archetype that mediates the development of consciousness. A strong ego-identity *precedes* the stage of a true initiate. Eros, as it develops from within, enables better inner and outer relatedness in the male. Anima is the root word in animosity and the moods of anima possession often include resentment. Men suffer at the hands of life until the anima forces the fact of life's power upon them. This greater conscious attitude, which may include acceptance and sacrifice, renunciation and resignation to life's forces, increases the sense of soul and leads to the wise old man, the archetype of meaning always standing behind the anima. Once the male attitude includes a freed-up anima, a man can relate to his own nature with a more integrated emotional attitude.

In the words of San Francisco analyst John Beebe:

> That Mercurius was for Jung the archetype of the unconscious tells us finally how masculine Jung's approach to the unconscious was. Despite his androgyny, Mercurius is a quintessentially masculine god, although not every masculinity will be grounded in this mythologem. . . . In the attributes of this god one can find Jung's own seminal ideas—the unconscious as an autonomous, creative being continually in motion between sets of opposites; the shifting shapes of the unconscious spirit as signals of its arrival at the gates of a different god; the trend of the unconscious toward stable wholeness within a contained intrapsychic life. Mercurius was . . . Jung's ultimate father-figure and masculine way through the psyche. His is the restless masculine spirit that informs. (Beebe 1989, xvi–xvii)

Live and let live seems to me the decent and sophisticated male opinion today as to what other men may wish to do with their sexual lives. The only truly interesting sexual act, I believe, is that which one is making oneself—whatever it may be. Pornographic voyeurism may excite the sexual organs to ejaculation rather than create a deep total orgasm which image and fantasy serve more to stimulate. In the animal kingdom, the males have seasons for sexual activity and seasons for sexual rest. Men need more complete sexual experiences, not so much constantly attempted unhappy sex. Men should make love only when psychically and physically they really want to and ignore the sexual patterns as to timing in other men's lives. Metabolism and sexual arousal patterns vary as much between men as the psychic aspects of what men like in bed vary. One makes one's own sexual life as best one can. Nature and nurture are involved in intrapsychic components of great complexity and variety. Temperament is involved with sexual patterns as is cold or warm climate, social ethics, need for fusion, relationship, and peak experience.

To deny sexuality its inherent place in the totality of a man's life can only bring havoc, suffering, and brutality forward in the world. Alienation goes with sexual repression. Open expression releases inherently varied sexual possibilities to more men. The sexual menu should be a varied choice with a loved partner and contain enough spirited nourishment in its wake to enhance selfhood and the feeling of being loving and loved. With the AIDS epidemic, the time of orgy and group sex must now somewhat wane into a condom-clad "safe sex" routine; men may now more often honor the joy of sexual relationship to a committed and truly loved partner. Sex is, no doubt, "what makes the world go round"! It should never be taken for granted just because it is available, but respected for its incredible personal, mutual, and cosmic peak experience. God must love sex very much to have made it so wonderful in human beings' lives!

An anonymous, sympathetic Scot summed it all up very neatly in the remark: "You should make a point of trying everything once, excepting incest and folk-dancing" (quoted in Sir Arnold Bax, *Farewell My Youth*, 1943).

I

The Alchemy of Masturbation

Just to stir things up seemed a great reward in itself.

Sallust, 86–35 B.C.

AUTOEROTICISM, as lone male masturbation, is a subject so widely neglected by psychologists that it makes one wonder why. Ninety-three percent of men have masturbated to orgasm at some time in their lives and a majority masturbate throughout life. This indicates that the power of the sexual urge is far beyond the expression of relationship to another person. Other forms of self-induced orgasm are rare, as only four men in every five thousand can achieve orgasm by fantasy alone, not touching the penis with their hands or other object of stimulation. Only three men in a thousand are gymnastic enough to be able to suck their own penises.

According to Heidenstram (1976), from whom I take my figures, masturbation continues to be used by 10% of married men throughout their sexual lives. This indicates that in intensity, feeling, and psychological impact, orgasm from the self-stimulation of the penis retains a significant range of experience not identical to, or replaced by, intercourse in all its variations with a partner. This has led me to look for an inner psychology such as alchemy to explain masturbation's power.

Masturbation begins very early in some infants, who stimulate themselves by rocking backwards and forwards on the genitals when less than one year old. From five years onwards autoeroticism may become more conscious; for the great majority of men, active masturbation to orgasm begins at thirteen or fourteen with the onset of puberty. The release of sexual tension and sperm production normally means that masturbation is the principal sexual outlet of early adolescence, a part of normal sexual experience. Among single men it continues as an outlet for up to 80%, particularly in the young and highly educated. Among married men, although the 10% incidence of masturbation is often accounted for by absence of the partner or other psychological difficulties and conflicts, I question that these reasons explain fully its continued presence. It would seem to me that psychology needs to look more profoundly at the inner self-expression that masturbation becomes for so many men, and take the whole subject much more seriously as a deep aspect of sexuality and psyche generally. Self-contained, self-enjoyed, self-stimulated phallic orgasmic ecstasy, the penis being stimulated by both hands and other objects or rubbed on other body parts, is a practice in literally billions of male lives. Why do we so rarely speak about masturbation as of natural psychological value, and as of great importance to male sexual life at all times and places where surveys about it have been conducted? Masturbation needs to be further raised to male consciousness. To do this I want to look briefly at aspects of its history. The history of masturbation has been engagingly described by James Hillman (1966). I want to bring forward again certain of his ideas on the subject in order both to agree and disagree. I will then extend my argument into an original contribution.

The history of both Jewish and Roman Catholic religious doctrine concerning masturbation was simply to condemn it. By the eighteenth century the influence of religion had made masturbation a sin and a crime; scientists had made it a medical disease. By the nineteenth century masturbation was described as a mental derangement by psychiatry. Incredibly, in female patients, epilepsy became linked to masturbatory practice, and clitoridectomies were performed for its relief! This brutal and blindly savage attitude in so-called scientific treatment, not to mention cultural attitudes, appears to have been based on a seed-loss theory. Apparently to have an orgasm alone defied God and caused epilepsy.

Prohibition of masturbation was finally challenged in 1912 at the first psychoanalytic conference on the subject, especially by Victor Tausk (see Reich 1951). Tausk described fantasy and guilt as primary psychological facts, and Freud's idea—that full discharge of pent-up sexual energy did not occur in masturbation, thus causing anxiety and neurasthenic neurosis—began to lose support. Almost forty years passed before Stekel (1951) declared the "disturbance" in masturbation to be unnecessary guilt feelings when inhibition failed to stop it. This was thought to connect fantasies of Oedipal conflicts with father or mother and with the superego incorporation of parental prohibitions towards childhood masturbation. Attitudes were finally moving towards a positive acceptance of masturbation as a norm in child and adolescent development. Kinsey (1948) had extended this to argue that adult masturbation is harmless and is not a substitute form of sexual behavior from heterosexual intercourse, but rather the second most often performed sexual activity, practiced by adults in parallel with heterosexual activity, and both preceding this activity in adolescence and often succeeding it in older age.

What is amazing historically is that until the twentieth century no one asked why the loss of semen should be harmful in masturbation but not in coitus. Even in sexual offenders, Gebhard reported that men jailed for rape, incest, sodomy, homosexuality, or child molesting, and who rarely admitted guilt about this, usually retained a separate anxiety about masturbating until they stopped it (Gebhard et al. 1965).

Even though psychology no longer believes masturbation to be regressive behavior or only a substitute for a partnered sexual act, there remains a widespread guilt reported in analytic patients by Mario Jacoby (1994, 86–7). This widespread attitude has led Hillman to propose an inhibition operating in psyche that is self-imposed by the general self-regulatory activity in psyche. He sees this as separate from the prohibition that until recently has come into the incorporation of strictures against masturbation from authorities such as parents and some of the religions. Freud believed that the lifting of this prohibition led to a "therapeutic return of masturbation" in patients who suffered from fundamental unease about the practice.

Hillman argues that prohibition only plays into an archetypal self-regulatory inhibition in the sexual instinct. He argues that within Jung's proposition that because a spectrum exists in the archetype of sexual instinct from an "infrared" primitive end through to a spiritualized "ultraviolet" end, he can place masturbation at the primitive "infrared" end of the spectrum as the cause of action. Here I want to argue differently, because the range of fantasies in masturbators' reports—from the pornographically induced infrared to highly oceanic, cosmic experiences of spirit at the ultraviolet end of the archetypal spectrum—make me doubt that an inhibition archetypally exists *a priori* to incorporated cultural and superego prohibitions. Fisher, Gross, and Zuch (1956) believe sexual excitation and its fantasy are one function in sexuality because penile erection in sleep coincides with the active dream cycle. Spitz (1962) reports that infants with good object relations to mothers or their surrogates masturbate more than deprived or isolated children. This supports my view that *outgoing instinctual relatedness leads to an auto-erotic celebration of an inner joy*. Unlike Hillman, I do not see masturbation as having an archetypal inhibition unless the damage to object relationships is at a very serious or catastrophic level, as Spitz implies.

I am arguing that the inventive, internalizing psychological experience of peak experience in relatively guilt-free masturbation is a paean of joy with its connections to fantasy creation, fire-making, and even shamanistic gifts. The Mojave Indian tribe consider frequent masturbation a childhood sign of a future shaman (see Devereux 1936). The religions have tended to try to suppress a person's creation of individual symbolism and its images. One of the most personal creators of symbolic image would be masturbatory fantasy. Duvall and Duvall (1961) tell us: "It is known that sexual behavior envisaged in daydreams or fantasy during masturbation will, in many cases, go far beyond any behavior the individual actually has experienced or wishes to experience in real life. This is especially true of males."

Perhaps because Western society so undervalues psychic life per se, we undervalue the positive psychological potential of masturbation, which I shall argue renews self-centering at a profound level and revitalizes psyche's self-regulation, neither more at home in body or spirit but alchemically and archetypally unifying both psyche and soma. Intrapsychic tension, powerfully sexually increased at adolescence in boys by the availability of semen production, is obviously released through masturbation; however, I believe psyche to relate this to an inner and creative potential which can be described as alchemical experience. I would wish in what now follows to raise this idea in the consciousness of my reader.

Before presenting my original analogy between alchemical process and masturbation's effects within psyche, I would like to defend analogy as scientific. In my book *The Self in Early Childhood*, I defended the use of the analogical act in psychological theoretical/experiential assertion as follows:

> Analogy, if presented in rigorous scientific and theoretical discussion, is heuristically useful. In the *New Oxford Dictionary*, one definition describes analogy as "the resemblance of form or function between organs which are essentially different." Where analogy is noticed, especially in medicine and biology, it is rarely carried through by logical argument in the step-by-step fashion of the philosopher. Much of the philosophy of science comprises theoretical situations that rarely happen in the real life of the laboratory or the clinic, and the term "analogical act" is considered more germane to my argument. Analogical acts are an aid to discovery because they suggest clues and hypotheses. They concern resemblances between the relationship of things, rather than between the things themselves. The value of even erroneously described analogues can be profitable, as it was with Malpighi: encountering insuperable difficulties in his anatomical studies of animals, he looked instead at their analogues, the plants, and founded the science of plant anatomy.

In biology and medicine, the examples of how analogies have helped new discoveries are legion. In neurophysiology these would include nervous transmission and electric current; the brain and electronic calculating machines; the eye and the photographic plate; and the study of memory, which employs many analogies in its understanding. The ancient Greeks (fifth century B.C.), who did not allow autopsies, used analogies in their attempts to understand the movement of body fluids, conception, respiration, nutrition, congestion and the formation of bladder stones. Descartes was concerned with the analogy between mechanical and physiological action, and analogy became the cornerstone of comparative anatomy.

Since analogies have a long history in generating hypotheses to inspire further investigation and development, it is scientifically justifiable to include the carefully argued analogues between masturbation and the alchemical process which follow. The analogical act never proves; it may, however, bring revolutionary advances if scientists detect certain analogies not seen by others, and thus give a new basis for further progress. (Ryce-Menuhin 1988, 162–3)

Masturbation as Alchemy

Alchemy has long been regarded as a symbolic precursor of the study of the unconscious and as an analytical approach to understanding a process of transformation within personality:

> The alchemists projected their internal processes into what they were doing, and, as they carried out their various operations, enjoyed deep, passionate emotional experiences along with spiritual ones. Critically, they did not attempt to split off experience from activity and in this way, too, they link with a contemporary psychological attitude, at least as interpreted retrospectively. (Samuels et al. 1986, 12)

In its own day, medieval alchemy was a secret and subversive practice, its images of fire, water, earth, and air a vivid contrast to the cold and sex-forbidden expression so stylized in medieval Christianity and later in Victorian times prior to Freud.

> As far as can be reconstructed, the alchemists of the fifteenth and sixteenth centuries had two interrelated aims: (a) to alter or transform base materials into something more valuable—variously referred to as gold, or a universal elixir or the philosopher's stone; (b) to transform base matter into spirit; in short, to free the soul. Conversely, the attempt was also made to translate what was in the alchemist's own soul into material form—his unconscious projections serving this need. These various goals may be seen as metaphors for psychological growth and development. (Samuels et al. 1986, 12)

The alchemist chose opposing elements to mix together seeking a new conjuncted substance which was pure. Because such a substance has never been found in nature, Jung approached alchemy from a symbolic viewpoint and found it a valuable analogous descriptive study for psychological consideration. Most alchemists were male and they often worked with a fantasy figure, a *soror mystica*, just as males when masturbating often fantasize a *soror sexualita* as their anima representation while erotically arousing self-stimulated sexual desire.

> The role of the "other" in psychological change is, by now, well known—Lacan's "stade du miroir" (1949) and Winnicott's emphasis on the mother's reflection to the infant of his integrity and worth (1967) are only two examples of this. Alchemy, therefore, straddles the interpersonal/intraphysic divide and is a metaphor which illuminates how a relationship with another person promotes internal growth, and also how intraphysic processes fuel personal relations. (Samuels et al. 1986, 13)

To seek the alchemical analogy to masturbation as opposed to having intercourse with an actual, not a fantasized partner, we have to seek categories of understanding as to how *psyche understands itself*. "Dissolve the matter in its own water" is one of the oldest common sayings attributed to medieval alchemists. Alchemical symbolism is so largely a product of unconscious psyche that it is only in projected images, as stages of alchemical process in masturbation, that we may find analogous ways to describe the process of masturbation.

In general, Jung believed projection was a means "by which the contents of the inner world are made available to ego-consciousness. The assumption is that an encounter between the ego and such unconscious contents is of value. . . . For anything of value to be gained, though, it is necessary for some re-integration or re-collection of that which is projected to take place" (Samuels et al. 1986, 13). In erotic sexual images during masturbation, a man can use projection to separate the subject (his pulsating erection) from the object (those fantasies that may include naked erotic images of an empathized partner or partners). Projection can draw in these erotic images to become a psychic part of the person masturbating. Empathy to the sexual image projection gives a kind of vicarious introspection, adding fuel to the sexual fire. Defensive control of the increasingly erect penis during masturbation enables a projective identification onto fantasized objects that tends to give one an impression that separation from the fantasized love object is almost eliminated.

In his study of alchemy, Jung found that a very luxuriant set of images became the psyche's "own water" or the way to understanding the complex nature of contents that are both conscious/unconscious in psyche. Jung wrote, "I was concerned with the interplay between conscious and unconscious, with the development of consciousness from the unconscious, and with the impact of the greater personality, the inner man, upon the life of every individual" (Jung 1961, 221; cited in Samuels et al. 1986, 13). What I now want to discuss are some of the ways that alchemical images can help us understand the feelings of transformation that masturbation can bring the self through its buildup to orgasmic peak experience. Alchemical symbolism can be regarded as mostly unconscious.

The real nature of matter was unknown to the alchemist: he knew it only in hints. In seeking to explore it he projected the unconscious into the darkness of matter in order to illuminate it. In order to explain the mystery of matter he projected yet another mystery—his own unknown psychic background—into what was to be explained. (Jung 1944, par. 345)

The "opus" or work of the alchemist was to connect or earth the more transpersonal symbolic elements that the evolution of consciousness demands our egos realize more fully. To become more, an individual symbolically continues to "create the world" as personality develops.

The freedom which the individual masturbator has to create the tempo of sexual arousal as his own idea gives a world-creating consciousness to him as he delays, during long masturbation, final arousal with wide variations of touch, thrust, fantasy, and will, in penis-play towards extremes of self-induced pleasure. This would be dangerously inflationary as one's sexuality becomes "the whole world" or the center of the universe, were it not so temporary and instinctively released in orgasm. The pouring forth of the "pure gold" of life-giving sperm as a *prima materia*, an *a priori* stuff or matter is not unlike, both when combined with woman's ovum and when not combined with it, a transcendent original substance of creation. As early as the pre-Socratic philosophers, thinkers searched for the so-called first matter. Thales named this "water," Anaximander named it *apeiron*, the boundless. Anasimenes named it "air," and Heraclitus called it "fire."

Edward Edinger described the *prima materia* of the alchemists as follows:

This idea of a single, original substance has no empirical source in the outer world. Externally the world is obviously a multiplicity. Thus, the idea must be a projection of the psychic fact. According to philosophical fantasy it was then imagined that the prime matter underwent a process of differentiation whereby it was separated into the four elements earth, air, fire and water. It was thought that these four elements then combined in various proportions to form all the physical objects of the world. Upon the *prima materia* was imposed, as it were, a fourfold structure, a cross, representing the four elements—two sets of contraries, earth and air, fire and water. Psychologically, this image corresponds to the creation of the ego out of the undifferentiated unconscious by the process of discriminating the four functions: thinking, feeling, sensation and intuition.

Aristotle elaborated the idea of the *prima materia* in connection with his distinction between matter and form. According to Aristotle, primary matter before it has been wedded to form or had form imposed upon it, is pure potentiality—not yet actualized because the actual does not exist until it has taken on a particular form. As one commentator of Aristotle puts it, "First matter is the name of that entirely indeterminate power of change" (Brehier 1965, 208).

The alchemists inherited the idea of *prima materia* from ancient philosophy and applied it to their attempts at the transformation of matter. They thought that in order to transform a given substance it must first be reduced or returned to its original, undifferentiated state. "Bodies cannot be changed except by reduction into their first matter" (Kelly 1893, 34). (Edinger 1978, 12–3)

This procedure reminds one of masturbatory excitement, because rigid or fixed aspects of personality are sexually transformed back toward their more primitive undifferentiated condition of ecstasy (paradise in the Garden of Eden) as the regressive pull which heralds the psychic transformation of deep orgasm. The body becomes a temple of passionate pleasure, almost innocent in its return to first sexual experience, autoeroticism, or masturbation.

The fragmented, disjointed condition of high sexual tension is generally discovered, when nearing masturbatory climax, to be multiple aspects of an underlying unity: the throwing together of the self in orgasm. This in itself, as sperm is ejaculated into the air, corresponds to a sense of the unconscious exposing of the ego to the infinite, the *apeiron*. "It may evoke the terror of dissolution of the awe of eternity. It provides a glimpse of the pleroma, the *increatum*, the chaos prior to the operation of World-creating Logos" (Edinger 1978, 15).

After the *prima materia* (such as sperm) is found, the alchemists went through a series of "operations" or chemical procedures in order to search for the final gold, the lapis, the

philosopher's stone, the pearl beyond price. These images
mean a unity, a oneness, an inescapable archetypal *unus
mundus*. The feeling at orgasm comes through several
clearly definable operations of alchemy: *calcinatio* (fire), *solutio* (water), *coagulatio* (earth), *sublimatio* (air), *circulatio*
(up and down circulation), and *coniunctio* (connection, or
the orgasmic feeling of unity to the world-creating World-
Creator) are some examples and possibilities.

Although each of these operations has an elaborate symbol system in myth, folklore, and religion, they have their
source in archetypal psyche. I shall be discussing the stages
of male masturbation as a corollary to the various alchemical categories as core sexual, instinctual stages of image and
symbol fantasy elements. Much has to be left unsaid on the
level of symbol and image which Jung defends in the spirit
of alchemical procedures:

> [W]e should not begrudge . . . the alchemists their secret
> language: deeper insight into the problems of psychic de-
> velopment soon teaches us how much better it is to re-
> serve judgment instead of prematurely announcing to all
> and sundry what's what. Of course we all have an under-
> standable desire for crystal clarity, but we are apt to forget
> that in psychic matters we are dealing with processes of
> experience, that is, with transformations which should
> never be given hard and fast names if their living move-
> ment is not to petrify into something static. The protean
> mythologem and the shimmering symbol express the
> processes of the psyche far more trenchantly and, in the
> end, far more clearly than the clearest concept; for the
> symbol not only conveys a visualization of the process
> but—and this is perhaps just as important—it also brings a
> re-experiencing of it, of that twilight which we can learn
> to understand only through inoffensive empathy, but
> which too much clarity only dispels. (Jung 1941, par. 199)

Calcinatio is a chemical process that entails the heating
of a solid in order to drive off water or any constituents that
will become volatile. In heating limestone to produce quicklime, when water is added quicklime generates heat. So in
rubbing the erect penis-shaft men usually use their spit, or
soft fluids like Vaseline, oils, or soap to generate further heat

to the erection. Urination is prevented once full erection is reached, so inner surfaces of erectile penile tissue are distended without much moisture in intense inner rubbing to equal the outer masturbatory friction from hands, body parts, or other objects used for stimulation like small air-filled cushions, pillows, or heated water-bags shaped like vaginas. To distend the penis to a rock-like solid, rubber coils can be slipped on the base of the penis to prevent the flow of blood leaving the shaft backwards.

The *Glory of the World* says, "Take fire, a quicklime of the sages, which is the vital fire of all trees [for example, erect penises], and therein doth God Himself burn by divine love" (Waite 1953). Fire has always symbolized libido (see Jung 1952, par. 208). In the fire of sexuality, the consciousness descends into the animal realm, where the fiery energies of instinct abide. In alchemical imagery the purification requires this fire, which is often symbolized by the lion or the egocentric sexual power drive. One moves back to the earliest ego stage of autoerotic desire. The power stage is moved through and sometimes temporarily halted by the various alchemical stages of masturbation to follow, the last of which, the *coniunctio*, leads to an augmented objective consciousness after sexual climax.

The full erection is now experienced in the first stage of frustrated fire-desire. In the fire, ashes build up. Ash is alchemically the equivalent of salt, which is found in high content in sperm. Salt has symbolized Eros, both as bitterness and as wisdom. *Calcinatio* is here likened to a drying-out process of the interior tissues of the penis between the engorged blood vessels, which dries out the urine-logged penis to become the phallic sun, the lion, the fire of male "pride," the "fucker," the "cock," the "prick," the "winger," the "rock." If shame, guilt, or anxiety were initially present in the masturbator, they now are "liberated" by the fire. A pure sense of joy, free of unconscious contamination, comes into psyche. The ego says "I want" and "I am entitled to." Inward body heat must meet the warmth of psychological acceptance at the start of masturbation to experience its alchemy, its purging and unifying effect and affect.

Solutio (or the solution) is at the root of alchemy. "Until all be made water, perform no operation" (Read 1963, 262).

"Dissolve and coagulate" sometimes sums up alchemy in a phrase. In giving way to sexual enjoyment, one needs to dissolve into a wet, womb-like attitude preparing for rebirth. An ancient text remarks, "Bodies cannot be changed except by reduction into their first matter" (Kelly 1893, 34).

Chemically, mercury must amalgamate with silver or gold, as the moon and the sun or the two highest vibrating metals. In masturbating, after full tumescence is reached, the next stage is the awareness of a soft internal juice just near the aperture of the penis head which will later enable the onrush of sperm without pain. Ego, or masculine sun, and the anima, or feminine moon, dissolve in the friendly water of the very matrix of the masculine sex, the erection maintained by slippery substances allowing both hands to grip the shaft as in a womb. The blissful state brings a uroboric incestuous feeling, passively giving way to the urgency of the erection, moving away from phallic thoughts to a temporary self-dissolution. Masturbation experienced underwater in baths or pools often is an aspect of this need for *solutio* practiced by some men when possible. As *solutio* takes over this stage of masturbation, the infantile ego is remembered, one "drowns" in a kind of original unknowingness. A sense of immersion in the creative flow of sexual libido develops. As this musing and unconscious stage proceeds there is danger of losing the erection, so the *coagulatio* stage must be reached before this happens. This may be aided by fantasies of naked females in their bath, for example, as in an Arab harem. The penis needs rejuvenation after almost dissolving into Eros, a softening process. One text says:

> You are to know that, although the solution is one, yet in it there may be distinguished a first, and a second. . . . The first solution is . . . the reduction of it to its First Matter: the second is that perfect solution of body and spirit at the same time, in which the solvent and the thing solved always abide together, and with this solution of the body there takes place simultaneously a consolidation of the spirit. (Waite 1953)

Coagulatio or earthing brings the mature ego back into the masturbatory sequence. The blood, directed by ego, surges even more into the erection which again takes one's whole attention. Bulging veins harden the exterior surface of the penis to a fuller distention. The head of the penis continues to enlarge. New rhythms of touching the penis such as squeezing, shaking, rolling, strumming, bouncing, and pulling bring an earth-totem feel to the rock-like penis in coagulation of inner and outer pressures. One senses the volcano of eruption in orgasm to come but holds back as the sexual-alchemical process continues.

Chemical reaction may produce a new solid compound when it is heated. Consider the egg white. When egg white is heated it coagulates into your breakfast "hard-boiled egg." So, too, the penis with renewed massage becomes a "hard-boiled penis." It no longer will change its shape until detumescence after orgasm. Ego-desire now fixes the penile erection into its final preprojective stage. There begins a countdown to final liftoff when autonomous processes will force ejaculation to occur.

At this stage the penis is like a churning rod. Edinger (1979, 27) points out that "there is an interesting *coagulatio* image in Hindu mythology. After the flood (*solutio*) which destroyed all men except Manu, the Hindu Noah, there was need to recover valuable things lost in the deluge. "Gods and genii churned the ocean of milk, using the great serpent (Sesa-naga) as a rope and the Slow-Mountain (Mandara) as a churning rod" (Danielou 1964). From this churning process various objects coagulated out like butter from cream. This same image is given a psychological application in the Upanishads. "Like the butter hidden in milk, pure consciousness (*vijnamam*—the state of Atman as Brahman, sheer bliss) resides in every human being. It is to be constantly churned, with the mind serving as the churning rod" (Zimmer 1952). This churning bliss was thought by Anaximander to be an external motion, like a vortex taking place in the "boundless (*apeiron*) of the *prima materia* of the alchemists' coagulation" (Burnet 1962, 52).

The substance the alchemists wished to coagulate was quicksilver or the spirit Mercurius (see Jung 1941, par. 239). This autonomous spirit of archetypal psyche, if subjected to *coagulatio*, connects the ego to the Self. In this momentous and forceful achievement, a person's psyche would rise up in a kind of *sublimatio*, the great mystery of alchemy, when it is said a shining white soul flies up to heaven with the spirit freed from the stone. Here we have a metaphor for the white sperm ejaculating free from the stone-like penis, as a release of the spirit hidden in matter. *Sublimatio* then is an expulsion or extraction from the very factuality of nature, and is here likened to the ejaculation of sperm at orgasm. *Sublimatio* to the alchemist meant the grinding or hammering of the material into well-pulverized or "fine bits." This image suggests the grinding and hammer-like grip of the hands on the penis at orgasm, throwing out sperm in "fine bits" of rhythmically tossed ejaculation. This is like spirit (the fecundity of the sperm cells) being separated from matter (the sperm production in the testicles).

The hammer or erect penis, just before ejaculation, feels remote from ego. The whole self experiences orgasm as if being thrown back into selfhood through ecstatic orgasmic unity with the One, with God's own eternal force of creativity. This restores an ego-Self balance which has varied throughout the stages of sexual buildup; the orgasm flies into the "air" or the *sublimatio*. The intensity of psychological awareness just after orgasm, suggests the accuracy of the renewal and rebirth elements of orgasmic awareness, so like the alchemical analogy of internal *coniunctio* as alchemy's constant goal.

Some men release their hands from the penis just before ejaculation to further experience a sensation of flying, soaring, or ascending, as if the soul were to reach Augustine's "heavenly Jerusalem." In a passage from Augustine's *Confessions*, he writes, "We ascend thy ladder which is in our heart, and we sing a canticle of degrees; we glow internally with thy fire—with thy good fire—and we go forward because we go up to the peace of Jerusalem" (13, 9).

> Upward movement eternalizes; downward movement personalizes. When these two movements are combined, we get another alchemical process, namely, *circulatio*. A paragraph from the *Emerald Tablet of Hermes* (see Atwood 1960) refers to *circulatio*: "It ascends from the earth to the heaven, and descends again to the earth, and receives the power of the above and the below. Then you will have the

glory of the whole world. Therefore all darkness will flee
from you." (Edinger 1980, 72)

The glorious inner and outer marriage to a cosmic maleness
in male *coniunctio* reveals a deep alchemical fantasy experience in masturbation.

A Note on Taoist Yogic Practice

Taoist yogic practices teach an ancient method of preventing
sperm from its ordinary course in sexual excitement, by
turning the generative force driven by sexual fire through
practices of regulated breathing into a microcosmic orbit.
This orbit begins at the base of the spine (Gate One) rising in
the backbone between the kidneys (Gate Two) and then to
the back of the head (Gate Three). It then reaches the brain
(Gate Four) and descends down the face (Gate Five), chest
(Gate Six), and abdomen (Gate Seven) to return to Gate One,
completing a full circuit. According to Lu K'uan Yu, a Chinese Buddhist whose first master was the Hutuktu of
Sikang, an enlightened lama, and whose second master was
the Venerable Chan Master Hsu Ysu Yuu—the Dharma-
successor of all five Ch'an sects of China—regulated deep
breathing reaches the lower abdomen to arouse an inner fire
which combines with the generative force. Both forces are
made to rise in the "spinal channel" of control to the head.
Out-breathing relaxes the lower abdomen, so that the fire
and generative force sink back into what is named the "front
channel" of function, moving from the head to the solar
plexus to the starting point at the base of the penis, to form
a full rotation of the microcosmic orbit. After cleansing
these forces to purification, they are held under the navel,
under and between the kidneys, an area which is linked both
to the brain and the soles of the feet, awaiting transmutation
into vitality. An alchemical agent is believed by Taoist yo-
gins to change the force in the solar plexus. This force rises
to the brain, controlled by well-regulated breathing, where it
transmutes into spirit. The detailed and complex practices

merely mentioned here receive a very complex description from the Taoist master Chao Pi Ch'en (b. 1860) in *The Secrets of Cultivation of Essential Nature and Eternal Life*. (An excellent translation and elucidation of this text is Lu K'uan Yu 1970.)

In Taoist yoga, all erections of the penis are quieted and ejaculation of sperm stopped by methods of yoga in a quest to strengthen life, or, in its ultimate form, to reach sainthood and immortality. Alchemically there are five elements: the element of metal (west) is related to passion, and the element of wood (east) to nature. Fire (south) is spirit, and water (north) is the generative force. The earth (center) is heart or thought (Lu 1970, 30).

> The four components concentrated upon by the adept are body, breath, incorporeal and corporeal souls symbolized respectively by the elements of water, fire, wood and metal of the four cardinal points of the microcosmic orbit: south, north, east and west. (The Chinese reverse the directions used in Western maps.) When the four unite with the element of earth at the center which stands for thought (concentration) this is called the harmony of the four components. (Lu 1970, 31n. 3)

It is stressed that the Taoist yogic practices of reversing sperm through breathing and meditation techniques—to control generative forces and connect to prenatal, not only postnatal spirit—should be learned only from a recognized master. It is claimed that the generative force can be fully sublimated within a hundred days and will then fill the lower abdomen. Through complex eye movements and breathing techniques it is claimed that prenatal vitality leads to a manifestation of original spirit or "that spirit of no spirit" (which is inexpressible). This produces what is named "the golden nectar" similar to medieval alchemists' gold. The Chinese Taoist yoga seeks in its alchemical body practices to produce the macrocosmic agent (golden nectar) by means of intercourse between positive yang and negative yin. For those men wishing to desist from sexual intercourse or masturbation to climax, Taoist yoga has much to offer. A teacher who is a master, however, is required.

In the West, celibacy has been the focus for the suppression of active, external sexual acts often, but not always, for religious reasons. The state of unmarried living has given rise to inner values, symbols, and images, especially in religious practice. In freeing the religious practitioner from the attractions and temptations of ordinary social/sexual life, it is believed that chastity may assist greater knowledge of an ultimate, mystical reality concerning the deity. A more profound level of holiness would be an aspiration of celibacy, seen either as a sacrifice of sexual desire in service to religious disciplining of mind and body as well as creating an unfettered availability for community service, or, as a symbol of innocence harking back symbolically to paradise, before evil and ambiguity developed socially around sexuality.

In Christianity, celibacy as an ideal has had a long history. During the first century, it is thought Syrian Christians made celibacy a requirement for baptism. Celibacy always related to attempts to clarify the role of the priest. Jesus mentioned celibacy as a virtue for some (Matt. 19:12) and St. Paul discusses it positively (1 Cor. 7:8–10). Celibacy was probably not obligatory for Christian clergy during the first Christian centuries, but Tertullian, Origen, and other writers of this early period mention it as widely practiced especially in monastic orders.

In the Eastern Christian church, marriage before ordination to the priesthood was allowed, but not after ordination. Later in the nineteenth and twentieth centuries, there was a move towards celibacy, following Rome, in certain eastern areas: Malabar, Syria, and the Coptic churches insisted on celibacy for their priesthood. In Spain, celibacy was practiced in the priesthood by the fourth century. During the Middle Ages, the French revived it when it quite widely lapsed. By the end of the twelfth century, the Catholic Church tried to enforce it generally for priests and nuns.

The Protestants in the Reformation broke away from celibacy, Luther and Calvin both denouncing it. The controversy increased also within the Catholic Church after the Vatican Council of 1869–70, as various Popes accepted areas where celibacy had been abolished, but by the reign of Pius XI, celibacy was again in place as a firm Catholic doctrine for the priesthood continuing to the present day. The institutionalization of celibacy indicates some protest against the excessive ties to the secular world expressed in religious congregations historically. Does spiritual authority increase in a celibate? The tension between priest and laity on this point has led to the powerful entrenchment of celibacy as an ideal in monastic life.

For Jungian psychology, however, celibacy has another strong meaning. The inner spiritual and imaginative union between man and woman may be symbolically strengthened by periods of celibacy in marriage. When refraining for a time from sexual intercourse, the internalization of the union may increase the couple's symbolic sense of a developing and continuing union, freed temporarily from its external, physically projected acting-out.

John Costello, a London analyst, has pointed out that the constant projection "out there" of sexual intercourse can be quite powerfully internalized during marital sexual abstention (1994). This can deepen the individual's sense of the development of the marital contract and the loving relationship as an image of inner union with the partner during periods of celibacy. Some persons will feel celibacy can aid this deepening spiritual awareness of their union with their partner; others may not feel this is necessary for their sense of the spiritual within the sexual.

The overall psychological power of the idea of celibacy, both within religious practice and within lay persons in society for whatever reason, give it a continuing credence in the lives of many men. In almost all known archaic cultures, chastity was practiced during times of war or drought, during mourning or special initiation rites, and during certain astrological periods. The purity associated with the idea of celibacy brought its orientation towards a psychological concept that celibacy deepens holiness, through a symbolic and a real awareness of the sacrifice of externalized desire towards a realization of an internal union or marriage to the ultimate spiritual value of ascetic, individual "inner marriage" of wholeness. Intermittent celibacy in marriage also can help a similar inner image of union to develop within each sexual partner, enabling a spiritualization and individuation to keep pace in development with periods of active sexual union alternating with periods of marital celibacy.

The knowledgeable alchemist will now ask, "All this feels right, but what about *nigredo* and masturbation?" *Nigredo* is the dark depressing time of import in alchemy when the shadow side of the personality may be confronted. In my clinical experience it is only younger men, aged seventeen to twenty, who, passionately desiring relationship during the height of their physical sexual drive, may descend into dark, earthy depressive feelings after masturbating. Men older than this experience not the regressive pull of a dark, moon-like face of negative mother in *nigredo* after masturbating, but report rather a sunlike, very masculine feeling of contentment, bodily relaxation, and an aftereffect of continuing pleasure. Many report an experience of spiritual renewal, healing, calm, and a conflict-free psyche.

This suggests to me that experience over time moves male masturbation through a regressive and remote past aspect of womblike *nigredo* feelings after orgasm in the late adolescent male, to a concentration in the adult male on the distal and proximal stimuli of intraorgasmic function covering all possible alchemical stages, other than *nigredo*. Where *nigredo* persists into later stages of life's development, this may suggest that separation from negative infant breast-feeding experiences with mother have not been reached. This can hinder a sense of genital freedom from psychological nourishment problems in experiencing self-induced sexual climax as solar, masculine, good self-feeding.

This does not need clinically to be interpreted as narcissistic, particularly when the entire psyche-soma may be involved at an instinctual level with feelings of numinous cosmic-mirroring at orgasm or before, not ego-induced mirroring fantasy as limiting or "separate." As long as billions of men continue to masturbate on planet Earth, we need to orient our Jungian sexual theories to this reality, giving masturbation the credence, honest airing, and theoretical/clinical ongoing analytic work which the phenomenon of its nature deserves.

II

Homosexuality—the Real Story

It is undoubtedly true that instinctuality conflicts with our moral views most frequently and most conspicuously in the realm of sex. The conflict between infantile instinctuality and ethics can never be avoided. It is, it seems to me, the *sine qua non* of psychic energy.

C. G. Jung

"WE HAVE BEEN PRIVILEGED to witness an evolution of attitudes about homosexuality in our time, mirrored in images as well as language. The label *queer* has been replaced by *gay* in public thinking and usage" (Beebe 1990, 111). The word "gay" may antedate the word "homosexual" by several centuries. Gay is now used "to describe persons who are conscious of erotic preference for their own gender" (Boswell 1980, 43). In the thirteenth and fourteenth centuries, the Provençal word "gai" came into use and survives in Catalan as meaning a lover, a "gaiol," an openly homosexual person. The south of France from that period onwards is noted for gay sexuality—especially the Albigensians who were referred to as "gaie." Many European languages earlier used "gay" to mean sexual "looseness" in general. Over time this term was attributed to homosexuals who were in more hostile environments than today. Boswell points out that its first public use ("gay" had long been a homosexual subculture code word) was in the 1939

Hollywood film, *Bringing Up Baby* when Cary Grant, wearing a dress, exclaimed he had "gone gay" (1980, 43n.6).

> Kinsey (1941, 1955) believed (like Freud) that humans are born with a capacity to respond erotically to either sex and that social factors dispose most people to prefer one to the other. . . . In this view, homosexual and heterosexual persons are representatives not of distinct types but simply of the end points on a sliding scale ranging from exclusive heterosexuality to exclusive homosexuality, with the majority of humans occurring at midpoints and capable of responding to either sex (but often constrained by circumstances to limit their responses to a single partner for much of their lives). If this view is correct, then *gay* people are those far enough toward the homosexual end of the Kinsey scale to think of themselves as chiefly homosexual. (Boswell 1980, 44n. 8)

I believe the etiology of homosexual feelings to be not yet fully understood. If homosexual preference can begin to develop in early infancy, its general intractability in analysis is understandable because it is both pre-Oedipal and pregenital. David Kay's description of "Harry's case" (Kay 1985, 45–68) describes homoerotic feelings building up in an infant son towards a father who did "bad mothering" during the mother's postnatal depression. This father exhibited an "almost psychotic delusional and intensely powerful quality" (64). The father's love fascinated the infant. This infantile fixation compelled Harry to search for a fusion to men in homosexuality as a grown man. Yet because these needs originated very early and are presexual in their fascination, the penetration by another male has given Harry no lasting satisfaction or feeling of ongoing relationship.

Where a bond to the mother continues with undiminished intensity on a son's part, Jung comments on a "secret conspiracy" between mother and son. In this situation, if there is an absence of an effectively strong father, Jung suggests that for a son to break free of his mother, "he would need a faithless Eros, one capable of forgetting his mother and undergoing the pain of relinquishing the first love of his life" (Jung 1950, par. 22). Anthony Stevens points out that analysis to free a boy from a powerful mother complex is very difficult (1990, 126–7). In any case the etiology of homosexuality remains less than clear. In studies between identical twins, there is a greater concordance for homosexuality than between fraternal twins, even when the identical twins are reared separately from each other. These reports are interesting, but still leave a nature/nurture controversy as to homosexual causation, for the foster parenting of the separated identical twins may have influenced homosexuality in unmeasured ways. Where cultural studies show a steady percentage of male homosexuality in a human population over generations, it seems impossible to separate the social factors from a possible genetic one. Statistics are not very reliable as often a much higher rate of homosexual experience exists in populations than males may admit to when questioned on the subject.

Alchemists have always believed that to join together consciously, a separation or deep perception of difference must occur. If a boy is too fused at infantile stages to either mother or father there is great danger to heterosexual development at puberty. John Beebe has rightfully pointed out that a man's anima development remains strong in his dreams and development through analysis whether the feminine image becomes projected and sexualized or not (1990, 96–111). This is true for both homosexual and heterosexual. While the anima remains for the homosexual a function of deep bridging to the core of self, it is expressed as a growing inner relationship "to his homosexuality as well as his lived relationships in the outer world with other homosexual men":

> Such development clearly parallels the anima's function of deepening the object relations of a heterosexual man and, just as in the heterosexual situation, to the degree that the homosexual man loves convention and his parents' values more than the relationship at hand, the anima will not develop. The homosexual's inner material like the heterosexual's will reveal a psyche stuck at some infantile, preadolescent, or adolescent stage of development in a classic mother or father complex. (Beebe 1990, 98–9)

Anima should be increasingly understood as that archetype in a man that when further known to ego through its images, will reveal a man's inner depths to himself. Often dreams will reenact fantasies that reflect a lived experience, a personification of the anima archetype. As homosexual men do not necessarily give the assignation of control of their unconscious to women (unless mother-bound) they may find a same-sex partner revealing their anima potential to them rather than assuming the usual male role of power dominance over them. Where a homosexual male experiences a man as an internalized healer, he may appropriate this image for the more usual image of woman as the internalized anima figure.

The Gay in History as Natural

It would seem to me that the greatest argument psychologically and historically about all types of male homosexuality is the question of whether gay sex is natural or unnatural. In an approach to this tricky subject, I want to look at some historical aspects of the gays and nongays of the European world and, later on, to look at some attributes and definitions of *nature* as such. Then I will deal with a psychodynamic view of gay sexuality.

In the early history of the Roman Empire we can find the foundations of the homosexual subculture. Whatever the atmospheric sense of antiquity that the word "homosexual" may draw up in the imagination, because of its association with Greek and Roman antiquity, the actual word homosexual was only coined late in the nineteenth century, most probably by John Addington-Symonds in his book, *A Problem in Modern Ethics* (1897, 1975). By the 1930s, the word homosexual replaced other earlier English words like inversion, intermediate sex, third sex, or homogenic love, and so on.

As I am not sure that the primary distinguishing characteristics of homosexuals is necessarily their sexuality (they may be much more interesting because of their talents, gifts, or their occasional genius), I prefer the use of the word *gay*, because it does not connote that such a man or woman is any more or less sexual than a so-called "straight" heterosexual (who may or may not be very sexual at all). The relative importance of overt sexuality, of love, affection, devotion, romance, and eroticism is something unique to each person, whatever their sexual preference in gender sameness or difference may be.

We know that in the ancient world, gay desire was considered entirely ordinary. Aristophanes of Byzantium characterized gay desire as a "natural necessity" or a part of human nature as strong as nongay desire, eating, drinking, or laughing (ed. 1885). Aristotle thought gay behavior natural since nature created both the statistically common and the less common in sexual preferences (1926). Plutarch thought that all humans are attracted to both sexes (1961), and Plato equated the idea of democracy with the acceptance of homosexuality in his *Symposium* (1932).

Aristotle makes the interesting point that when the Cretan lawmakers accorded public honor to gay sexuality among the Celts (the barbarians of the time), it had the effect on society of reducing attachment to wealth. To some extent, British concepts today have a parallel. It is curious that Britain legalized gay sex between consenting adults at roughly the same period as their flirtation with overt socialism after World War II, thus loosening the anality the Empire had always collectively expressed in its use of and retention of money. Material inflation has now changed this, since 1970, and the media denigration of certain gay persons in high places has developed, against the legal position of Britain, in the last ten years. This seems to uphold Aristotle's theory about the relation to money in society (now rather retentive once more) and the acceptance of gay sexuality. However, in the richest nation of all, the United States, the attachment to wealth is continued with a liberal attitude to gays. According to Kinsey's study (1948), statistics throw confusion onto the Aristotelian theory, as 13% of adult males and 7% of adult females are primarily gay and 40% of the male population and 20% of the female population have had some overt gay sex after puberty in the United States.

If history affirms that a majority of males were gay in ancient Greece, gay feelings in Rome seem to have been only a part of the erotic life of the time, although clearly documented to have existed very commonly at all social levels. Edward Gibbon (1898) thought that only one of the first fifteen emperors of the Roman Empire was not gay, or that for two hundred years the rulers of Rome had strong gay interests.

The first law, not too clearly made against gay sex, came in around 226 B.C. This law is so obscure no one knows clearly what form it took or whether it was actually used or enforced. Early imperial Rome can be seen as a base period for the social tolerance of gay identity or gay activity in the West. An indifference to gender in sexual interest is simply taken for granted in all the texts of this period, according to today's most eminent authority on the history of the gays in early Europe—John Boswell, an assistant professor of history at Yale University (see Boswell 1977, 1980). It was only in the fifth century A.D. that homosexuality was described as an inherited or incurable disease and more derogatory words against gays as a class developed in the literature. Nevertheless, Roman society never apparently exhibited as a whole such a lack of tolerance for sexual preference as have its European heirs.

As we move to the early Middle Ages we might pause to think about the confusion that Christianity brought to the morality of homosexuality. St. Paul decried homosexual acts as such, but he never criticized gay persons as such (see Boswell 1980, 335–53). Christ never mentions homosexuality, but speaks of love when He refers to St. John, probably His closest male friend. I have no reason to think that Jesus was not celibate—it has often, but not always, been the mode of the avatars.

The interpretation of the destruction of Sodom that Jesus gave was simply one of inhospitality. He indicates that ultimately social groups who isolate themselves as separate, chosen, or exclusive will be destroyed by the wrath of God. In Jewish tradition, the legend had the women of Sodom having intercourse with the angels. References to pride, that most exclusive of sins, occur regularly in the Old Testament as a reason that God abhorred the Sodomites—

plus greed, gluttony, idleness, and lack of generosity. All this is confused because the word for homosexual relations in Latin became *sodomita* in the Middle Ages. When angels were sent to investigate Sodom, Lot entertained them without the permission of the elders, who traditionally controlled who could stay over within the city walls at night. There is confusion about what transpired when the men of the city demanded the visitors come out so they could "know" them. It seems remote that seeing who they were implies homosexual rape. In only ten of 943 occurrences in the Bible does the Hebrew verb "to know" have anything to do with carnality.

The only place the Old Testament actually speaks explicitly against homosexuality is in Leviticus 18:22: "Thou shalt not lie with mankind, as with womankind: it is abomination," and, in Leviticus 20:13, "If a man also lie with mankind, as he lieth with a woman, both of them have committed an abomination: they shall surely be put to death; their blood shall be upon them." I presume lesbianism was left aside because of the very low status of female children in the Jewish tribes. Their sexuality was not even worth proscribing in the book of faith.

By the seventh century, sodomy referred to so-called unnatural sexual acts of any kind, such as heterosexual anal intercourse as well as gay sex. Through their rituals, the Jews always tried hard to separate themselves from neighboring Arab tribes, and it is important that no less a Biblical interpreter than Maimonides thought that the above-quoted passages from Leviticus (which occur in the context of other prohibitions against incest and adultery as well as gay sex), reflected the usual need for Jews to announce themselves as distinctive—a pride that has cost them dearly (see Maimonides 1965 ed.). Ceremonial uncleanliness is proscribed in the Bible, but inherent evil seemed more connected in the words of St. Paul and Jesus with the failure to keep the interior soul in perfect fidelity with the ethical heritage of the group.

Non-Jewish converts to Christianity were made exempt from much of Jewish law at the Council of Jerusalem (c. 49 A.D.). Four Mosaic laws were kept for all: to abstain from pollution of idols, from bloodshed, from things strangled, and from fornication. In Greek translations of the Bible, homosexuality is subsumed under the Greek word for adultery, not the Greek word for fornication; so, at the Council of Jerusalem, gay sex is just not mentioned as having a law for pagan converts to Christianity. Roman law and the law of Israel really had very little to say about gay sex. St. Paul seems to criticize heterosexuals who engage in periodic homosexual behavior more than he does permanently gay persons, in the same sense that he hated Romans for rejecting monotheism.

Translations have confused something else that is very important. The Greek phrase translated into English as "against nature" was first used by Plato. It meant the ethnic character of a person or a group—the word "nature" was always used with a possessive such as in "someone's nature," either the "nature" of the Jews or Gentiles, or that of the pagan gods. After two thousand years the use of the word "natural" or "nature" has been very much changed with its associations to social taboos, its patristic and Reformation theology, its didactic use in Freudian psychology, and all sorts of personal misgivings that abound in historical writers. The concept of a natural law, such as whatever that may mean in Jung's belief that psyche is teleological in its development and process, was not developed as a use of language until one thousand years after St. Paul's death.

That something is against nature, as a Biblical idea, really seems to mean any behavior that is unexpected, or different from the most statistically common. There is very little support for a translation of "immoral" with respect to homosexuality. One might say that gay sex was seen by St. Paul as beyond nature, in the sense of "peculiar" or "extraordinary," and perhaps as a way of expressing sexuality that was somewhat obsessive. Any connection between sex and procreation came along well after the Biblical sources. Until the twelfth century, there was no concept of "falling in love," or the romantic and passionate love which came to be a common basis for marriage in industrialized societies. Marriage laws, until the Industrial Revolution, were involved with a newer monogamous sexual morality within societies where social services did not yet exist for orphans or widows, unwed mothers, or divorcées. Neither, for that matter, did birth control exist except by way of abstinence, abandonment of unwanted children, or abortion. The New Testament offers a crude outline for social action and offers no complete or clear sexual ethic. Jesus always made social answers to immediate questions asked of Him. The remarks of Jesus on familial love appear to be negative, although his attitude is stronger concerning clan or tribal commitment than on family. Jesus thought friendship the highest form of human commitment, and took no recorded stand on gay sex.

Why then is there so much hostility to gays among Christians? This hostility probably grew fervidly when the Roman dissolution occured, that is, the time from the third through sixth centuries when increased bureaucratic control of personal morality, plus public pressure toward hypocrisy in sexual matters, led to criticism of homosexuality. Freud was to break through this only fourteen centuries later! During the Middle Ages, clerics often expressed homosexual love more often than did the poets. This changed in the eleventh century, when gay literature was established and survived, partly because gays became influential and prominent in the cultural achievements within both religious and secular life. The public finally became interested then in gay persons. Examples of this interest in personalities are Virgil and Plutarch, read to the present day; Alcuin, who presided over Charlemagne's court; Walafrid, the Abbot of Reichenau; Bazzi, the Italian Renaissance painter; al-Mutamid, king of Seville, and al-Mutamin, king of Saragossa, each of whom had Christian male lovers in the eleventh century; and, Ibn al-Farra, a court teacher of the Qur'an in Almería.

Up to this time, probably the most influential definition concerning "nature" and the "natural" had been that of Boethius, who died in 525 A.D. (see Boethius n.d., *Patrologiae*, 64). He wrote that (1) everything that exists is nature; (2) nature is all that acts or is acted upon; (3) nature includes all the principles of motion; and, (4) the inherent quality of something is its nature. The first three meanings fit gay sex, and, if homosexuality is considered partly innate by some, then the inherent meaning may be suitable to some gays. Later, in the ninth century, Eriugena wrote, "Nature . . . is the general name for everything which is and is not. . . . Nothing at all can be conceived of which would not be comprised by this term" (see 1968 ed.).

With the late twelfth century, a virulent hostility to gays developed within a general intolerance to minority groups, and was expressed by public and religious institutions. The Crusades against non-Christians, the expulsion and murder of Jews in Europe, and the Inquisition all remind us of the ferocity of this new, fanatical intolerance of minority status in whatever form it cropped up. Philosophically, it is difficult to know how majorities treat homosexuality as unnatural, if we remember Eriugena's four species of the "genus" of nature:

> *That which creates and is not created* (example: the end of
>   a species, which the Wildlife Trust tries to foster and
>   preserve);
> *That which is created and also creates* (heterosexual pro-
>   creative conception through intercourse);
> *That which is created and does not create* (homosexual in-
>   tercourse);
> *That which neither creates nor is created* (as our knowl-
>   edge is hardly cosmic knowledge, there may or may not
>   be such a constituent in nature. We cannot yet measure
>   the extreme slowness of cellular vibration in particles of
>   rock to see if they are "living" in this sense, for example).

I would like to turn now to some psychodynamic ideas about homosexuality in men.

The Gay in Depth Psychology

We have Freud to thank for the general acceptance of all forms of sexuality. Homosexuality is psychologically distinguished from neuroses, psychoses, and character disorders by the Freudians, although these conditions may coincide and interact with aspects of sexuality. Where gay sex is deviant from heterosexual coitus with orgasm, Freudians believe there is a regression to aspects of sexual foreplay that involve the basic instinctual drives and the sexual part object, or the whole sexual object. A return to early childhood sucking, excreting, and masturbating mechanisms is often involved in psyche, and sometimes an intense identification with opposite gender sexual behavior patterns is introjected. Let us examine Freudian theory more closely.

Freud's libido theory sees somewhat different drive aims in homosexuality from heterosexuality, and studies this separately from the differences in body-gender and orifice choices involved. It is clear that in the gay world, "The erotic expression of the sexual deviant is an essential feature of his psychic stability and much of his life revolves around it" (McDougall 1972). Fenichel (1945) thought that genital primacy was disturbed in the gay person, and that a partial component in foreplay dominates over pleasure in the sexual act itself. Although this leads to an apparently "neat" theory—that as genital primacy during a child's phallic phase (Oedipal complex) is commencing, a castration anxiety interferes with genital primacy—there remains a problem for this theory in much gay experience. In clinical practice there is evidence that in anal intercourse, the sexual orgasm is the prime genital aim, exactly as in vaginal penetration, so that castration complex theories thought of as destructive to genital primacy become more questionable a claim.

This is especially so as many homosexual partners alternate between receiving anally or orally the partner's erection while masturbating themselves, and then reversing the roles and actively penetrating the partner's anus or mouth as a symbolic vagina. Balint (1965) has better understood that genital pleasure has primacy in homosexuality and that all forms of coital orgasm require some regression in any case. In general it would seem that all the loving and hating towards parents in the early pre-genital and Oedipal phase of childhood is where defenses about aggression get tied into sexual object choices. Identification conflicts which a child experiences with parental figures seem to influence masculine/feminine identity aims, with the question still remaining open as to how a boy's need to protect his genitals and to feel his penis as absolutely primal to his nature, pride, and sexual pleasures, turns into castration anxiety. It is true that some boys feel shock when they first find the penis missing in girls, which would support a castration anxiety theory, but many boys simply experience fascination and a "sexual blush" throughout their bodies when they first see or feel a vagina. The Oedipal rivalry with father for intimate possession of mother may contain desires to castrate the father. The fear of retaliatory punishment would give guilt and anxiety but many boys esteem and love their fathers sufficiently never to desire their castration, even if the boy's mother-love is powerful. If identification to mother is sexually overwhelming, then father may become fantasized as the preferred partner in a secondary development within the boy to "become" mother, and the roots of gay sex may be sown.

Another aspect of the problem involves intense narcissism. Freud (1914) comments helpfully:

> We have discovered, especially clearly in people where libidinal development has suffered some disturbance . . . that in their later choice of love partners they have taken as a model not their mother but their own selves. They are plainly seeking *themselves* as a love-object and are exhibiting a type of object-choice which must be termed "narcissistic." In this observation we have the strongest reasons which have led us to adopt the hypothesis of narcissism.

Self-representation in narcissism could be said to neutralize drive energies or turn them, as in some gays, to a need for a male body almost identical to their own, a kind of self-twin. One can also observe some heterosexual partners who look like twins.

Where a mother rejects her child's narcissistic needs through a lack of empathy, the child will repress his own needs as they are not mirrored to him, resulting, by the time adulthood is reached, in an ego-splitting which drains off ego energies. To substitute for this lowering of self-esteem through ego expression, Kohut (1970) has shown how gay fantasy can act as a regulator of inner esteem, replacing a stable or less eroticized value system. I quote Rosen (1979) who has effectively summarized Kohut's male patient's case as follows:

> This case presented for treatment because of homosexual fantasies. The fantasies were understood in the analysis as

"sexualized statements about his narcissistic disturbance," and "stood, of course, in opposition to meaningful insight and progress since they were in the service of pleasure gain and provided an escape route from narcissistic tensions." Kohut showed how in this case where there was no acting-out of the fantasies, the sexualization of the patient's defects was due to a moderate weakness in his basic psychic structure, resulting in an impairment of its neutralizing capacity. The fantasies themselves, which occasionally led to orgasm, were of a quasi-sadistic triumph over men of great strength and of perfect physique in which they were rendered helpless or drained of their power by him masturbating them. . . . [The patient] had in his sexual fantasies replaced the inner ideal with its sexualized external precursor, an athletic powerful man; and he had substituted for the enhancement of self-esteem, which is experienced by living up to the example of one's idealized values and standards, the sexualized feeling of triumph, as he robbed the external ideal of its power and perfection and thus in his fantasy acquired these qualities for himself and achieved a temporary feeling of narcissistic balance. The specific pathogenic disturbance in this patient related to the traumatic devaluation of the father-image and its idealized aspects of the beginning of latency. This occurred on an earlier basis of an assumed failure of his mother to supply proper empathic responses to him early in life based on her unpredictability and shallowness. (Rosen 1979, 70)

Kernberg (1975) has stressed that where a mother has not given the male baby sufficient oral satisfaction at the breast, a boy may fantasize a sexual submission to father. Rage that may surround such feelings is both projected and introjected in ways which may split and threaten the internalized images of both mother and father.

Gay sex is often a defense against this internal image confusion, with a phallic overvaluation that results in a desire both to project and be protected by the partner's penis—a projection/introjection of phallic intensity. Conflicts over weaning in infancy which feel like injury can lead the gay to defend as well against a depression over the loss of mother's breast. Where potency is lost in very passive gays, the potency is reinstated psychologically by receiving the partner's erection and orgasm. These recessive gay types often safeguard against apathy and despair by acting as the "good mother" to their partners.

To the extent that a homosexual solution in psyche is often a defense to lessen anxiety or to create barriers against conflict, it gives the sense of survival. Paranoid anxiety may suggest that the gay fears *psychological* castration by men and women alike. Introjecting persecutory experiences may cause defense against unwanted parts of oneself to project again outwards. To appease this aggression, two gay behaviors can occur: the one, a hostile and greedy oral impulse against the partner, so that they are retaliatory; and the other, an appeasement of this need by submitting to anal intercourse and then reassuring themselves in giving gentle, non-biting fellatio to their partner, that their biting and destructive impulses (towards mother's breast and father's penis) are under control and no longer devouring.

In Jungian psychology, sexuality is seen as an archetypal system, not only as an instinctual drive aim. "Archetypes are innate neuropsychic centres possessing the capacity to initiate, control and mediate the common behavioural characteristics and typical experiences of all human beings irrespective of race, culture or creed" (Stevens 1982). When one considers the erotic in dreams, daydreams, subliminal advertising, and pleasure seeking, it becomes clear that procreation is an "artifact of sexuality, since people seldom . . . mix sexual enjoyment with the conscious intent to produce offspring. Sexuality is every bit as much concerned with pleasure and with bonding as it is with procreation" (Stevens 1982, 196). Our ego freedom, which is based on our specifically developed human frontal cortex, gives us a wide choice within the archetypal programs we actually live out sexually in our lives.

As the sexual potential of self is developmentally so varied, gays experience in their partnerships the progress of individuation, or the most acute possible actualization of the self, through the symbolic projection onto partners of that which they seek. Through the attachment, each lover unconsciously assists his partner to grow in the way that the lover already has, and to further bring into consciousness potentials for individuation. One might argue that gays are making up for an inadequately masculine father figure on which they can model their own masculinity. With the delay of this development it becomes reinforced and sexualized to other males. Where a boy is left *uninitiated* to the masculine world because of his father's selfish absence of influence and prototypical image-building, he will seek these qualities in another available male and may also allow his mother complex to dominate his general temperament at the same time.

The masculine principle seems to need trials and ordeal, such as separation from mother during early puberty, fully to actualize its relative growth within selfhood. Stevens goes so far as to assert that the Self archetype anticipates "that some form of initiation procedure will be vested in the culture" (1982, 158). Where society has few if any puberty rites, as in Western society, males will not be able to experience a fully actualized masculine principle. Where a pubertal boy sets up his own initiation complex to compensate for a culturally instigated one that is missing, that complex tends to become eroticized. A gay masochist will put himself through abuse and submission to a gay "master" and remain stuck in the repetition of this erotic ritual. The gay sadist will project his latent and uninitiated sexual potential in painful acts made onto a sexual partner, as if he were symbolically initiating himself in this erotic sequence of sexual domination and pain infliction.

What about the powerful image of the penis as a trigger in homosexual development, the penis that is *not* father's? The initiation of homosexuality may begin when a boy of under seven years for the first time in his life sees a man who is not a family member naked. This "otherness" of adult male pubic hair, large genitals (to a child's eye), and bodily muscular power can set up an image in a very young boy that may become erotically introjected into the growing child's fantasies. He cannot wait to become adult and, in the years prior to puberty, he may aspire and hold to this image and gradually long to be like the internalized image. If this image becomes eroticized, it may delay his own full sense of maleness when puberty arrives, with its breaking voice and its awkward preview of manhood. He may still want to be the internalized image, and the desire for this sameness may lead to homosexual experimentation. Where a strong-willed mother has demanded much of a boy's time and attention when he is not at school, he may need to escape feminine interference; a fear of feminine influence may lead to homosexuality, a world free of woman's external presence and internal pressures.

I do not refer here, when thinking about homosexuality, to masturbatory experimentation between boys of the same age at puberty, which may enhance each boy's feelings of masculinity by their temporarily sensing other male sex drives and realizing each one's own sexual powers. When this mutual masturbatory experimentation is not personalized, and penetration of mouth or anus is not attempted, homosexuality is not particularly present and usually an intense heterosexuality soon becomes apparent. This experimentation is forgotten and serves as a stimulus merely to penis-pride. But where older, admired males seduce young adolescents, the beginning of a clear pattern of homosexual activity emerges. Subsequent behavior can depend on the nature of this early same-gender sexual experience, the psychical and physical levels of pleasure initially experienced that may determine the course of a male's sex life. Often, it leads to a strong change, where heterosexual drives in the boy are established, homosexuality is rejected, and may never return.

Where male-to-male passion is established, however, and where sexual acts become powerfully exciting, the mania of promiscuous homosexuality may follow. In the active homosexual, statistics suggest that one thousand partners are often tried out before a homosexual settles to one or a few partners. What is the frenzy about? For some, it is a search for a larger penis or a more athletic or classical body. It has little to do with the person otherwise: part-object obsessions lead to "one-night stands" where a ritual of silent or quick seduction takes place. The place where sex is ritualized may indicate fixations onto public danger, such as seduction in public toilets, darkened public theatres, or public parks. Here the fear of police apprehension adds to the excitement. Usually, this sexual ritual is accelerated, and often remains a "quick fuck," between one active and one passive partner.

Where privacy is attained in hotel or apartment bedrooms, the gay sexual one-night stand may contain fuller expression on the part of both partners; both may penetrate each other successfully and full orgasms may be attained, not just quick ejaculations. Fantasies, usually sado-masochistic in character, may be acted out at varying levels of intensity. Patients who are homosexually promiscuous rarely speak of love or even affection—sexual cooperation seems enough to them, and their diaries merely record Christian names of partners, the type of physical acts experienced, and perhaps a telephone number; but usually not even the possibility of repeated contact is wanted. In the frenzied pickups, there seems to be a celebration of the male body, an evocation of collective ecstasy in bodily function, but without further attraction, repetition with the same person, or need for an intimate understanding of another's personality. Depression often follows, which is then defended against by another sexual experience with another stranger. Often, the general image and physical type of the selected partner resembles the first naked man other than a relative seen in childhood. Before puberty, this image from childhood often becomes an image sought after in bed. Erection of the penis, or penetration of the anus or mouth by one or both partners, stimulates the imagination further, but never seems to be replaced permanently by the reality of the actual partners seduced.

When values of mutual responsibility and shared interests may arise, promiscuous homosexuals may slow down and finally settle, usually with difficulty, to one partner. During middle age, these homosexual marriages often feel tenuous because so many younger men are admired, or "waiting in the wings," hoping to break up these marriages. "Open" homosexual marriages, encouraging outside sexual affairs, have about as much success as do "open" heterosexual marriages—in my experience, about 80% of these marriages break up, as opposed to about 35% of "closed" marriages, heterosexual or homosexual.

During my years of work in the arts and in the analyst's chair, I have remarked that various impressions of homosexuals arise in the conversations and experiences of heterosexual men, with regard to the behavior of gay men. Such reports from heterosexuals have taken on an almost predictable summarial view of homosexuals. Many consider that, to one's face, homosexual men are much nicer, more civilized, and more generous than heterosexuals—that homosexuals are nicer to deal with in person, face-to-face. This favorable impression is then leavened by heterosexuals' belief that they fare less well later, that behind one's back, aggression, envy, and hostility can arise even more quickly in homosexuals than in heterosexual men.

The "cloning" tendency in recent years is difficult to understand. The look-alike appearance of gay clones of the 1980s and 1990s has a curious persona look-alike which seems to ape the movie stars of the 1940s in the United States. The projected narcissism of wanting to be a look-alike strikes me as a negation of individuality that is sad to behold. At a time when both legally and socially in cosmopolitan society, homosexuals are accepted more than in earlier times in this century, the militant tendency to appear the same as their fellow-travelers strikes me as self-destructive and lacking in imagination. Among gays, however, a sense of proud "liberation" is often reported, a sense of inner freedom in being a "clone"—the opposite of appearances.

The penis cult remains rife among many gays. They constantly seem to speak about penises as, often, heterosexuals will speak about nothing but women's breasts. Certainly, sucking penises suggests breasts cannot nourish enough, and that milk—in the guise of sperm—needs ever to be ejaculated, ever an expression of "nourishment" for the homosexual. The anus takes on the unspoken mystery in the gay world that the vagina exemplifies in the heterosexual world. Of course, jokes about these body parts are constantly the cover-up for the sense of mystery that men tend to experience just as they proceed to penetrate the anus or the vagina.

The body heat of the male anus exceeds the body heat of the woman's vagina at climax; some men find this heat the deep, lustful, animal reason for preferring penetration of the male anus to all other penetrative possibilities in nature. With the AIDS epidemic, the use of condoms lessens the transmission of body heat and considerably cuts some aspects of physical pleasure. Condoms are much too tight for average or above-average sized penises, and constrict pleasure points considerably in the forward part of the shaft. It is surprising that better condoms have not yet been marketed now that the commercial market is wide open for huge sales and improvements.

The penis cult has led gays to a greater foreplay with testicles than most heterosexuals receive from women. Masters and Johnson have reported in detail about this fact (1979). An empathic knowledge of how testicles can be stimulated in foreplay is shared by men and, in this aspect, gays are expert in humorous, skillful sexual excitation of testicles in preparation for a maximum erection. Women less often find testicles an important part of their attraction within foreplay, and tend to concentrate more on the penis, nipples, neck, and lips of the male partner. Foreplay with the anus seems to be very familiar to foreplay with the vagina. This is perhaps one area of similarity in the active bisexual man from the point of view of physical techniques in sexual foreplay.

Psychologically, however, a very different world of inner and outer images must be available to the male bisexual. Skin oil, texture, and odor are very different in men and women. Muscle tone, lower body structure, and angles of coital movement vary between men and women. The outer surface of the anus is tight, and entrance to the anus requires delays as the anus lips expand more slowly than the outer lips of the vagina in experienced partners. Depending on coital positions in anal sex, gays may find deep mouth kissing simultaneous with orgasm impossible due to body angles in face-to-face anal sex.

One of the greatest debates today is whether body orifices are polyvalent and that therefore bisexuality is completely "normal," or whether a regression is present where oral or anal sex is used (whether gay or heterosexual). It is unclear to me what reasoning is used when regression is claimed in using some orifices and not others; the fact that sucking the breast nipple is the earliest reflexive experience for food absorption and then the anus expels solids soon after does not mean that the penis is available for erection at first in the baby when mouth and anus begin to function. So the relation between mouth, anus, and vagina as they relate to the penis is much more complicated than a theory of regression. As the penis requires a warm rubbing from a comfortable surface for its build-up to orgasmic ejaculation, the hand, the vagina, the anus, and the mouth—although these are all body parts that have other functions (as does the penis)—can function to give the penis erectile support in coital sexual movement. Persons who prefer one method of sexual build-up of erectile tension as opposed to another may not be regressed but merely adept at a particular way of stimulation.

Psychic images during sex are so varied in reports that no claim could be made that one form of sexual stimulation is more "mature" than another. Obviously, for natural procreation, heterosexual genital sex is necessary. Does this make it superior, however, for any other absolute psychological reason? I suspect not. The polymorphous aspect of the body parts used in all forms of coition suggests such a view is inaccurate, and a dangerous underevaluation of the range of content during human sexual acts to consider a theory of regression—in terms of the body orifices used sexually—to have any vital credence whatsoever to male sexual psychology.

Sexual play and the ecstasy it can produce in peak experience is what needs to be considered. Men experience a "throwing-together" of the self in sexual climax. Heterosexual men report feeling cosmic consciousness during coition well before orgasm. They feel one with yin and yang. Homosexuals refer more to the ecstasy of sameness they feel as they introject their partner's more similar ecstasy and project it psychologically back to him. More published report is needed about this aspect and contrast between gays and straights. It is unclear to what extent the psychic content of the question of whether one chooses to be gay or not could be affected if men shared the psychological aspect of their sexual experiences more fully with the world.

The idea that one is born homosexual seems to be a difficult question. There is a wide body of literature trying to confirm a hereditary influence in homosexuality. But the results of mammalian experiments, of the gay twins studies who are reared apart, and the studies of cellular differences found in the hypothalamus of gays and nongays who have died of AIDS are all contaminated by so many uncontrolled and abnormal factors and influences not tested that there is not enough hard scientific evidence to justify the arguments against *nurture as the dominant role in the development of gay sex preferences.*

The striking fact has emerged from laboratory studies in general that the psychological, sexual, and even gender role

> coincides in the majority of instances with the assigned sex and type of rearing. It would seem from these studies that the human infant's orientation as a male or female does not depend solely on the chromosomal and hormonal factors . . . but also on the psychological experience of being reared as, and regarded as, a boy or a girl. (Michael and Zumpe 1979, 456–7)

Laboratory experiments on rats do show that if stress occurs to the mother while a male is *in utero,* such as deprivation or reduction of androgen in the perinatal period (days fourteen to twenty-one of gestation), males are both demasculinized and feminized while the female litter-siblings are hardly affected. Could there be a special vulnerability to the human male's sexual behavior patterns from stress *in utero,* and does this lead to a propensity for gay development? We simply do not know at this time.

Males appear to be either "pushed" into homosexuality or not by early availability and partial proclivity to sexual play with other males; first positive or negative same-gender sex experiences and decisions as to lifestyles contain elements that accompany and enhance sexual choices. These experiences influence a man's choice as to whether gay sex will enter or remain a part of his sexual pattern. We know that, since Jung's time, research into male homosexuality suggests gay mental illness is more caused by homophobia, the hatred and fear of homosexuals by others, than by anything inherent in homosexuality itself. Therefore causation has become less interesting to research than the phenomenology of homosexuality. Jung had three causative ideas, however. One was that homosexuality is nearly always a result of a particular relationship with the feminine, often an unresolved dependence on the personal mother. Jung saw gays as acting out an identification with their own anima and projecting their personas on same-sex partners.

One problem with this is that it tends to put gays into an

immature or infantile dependence on the unresolved feminine connection, an attitude not accepted so widely today.
One of its problems is that male-to-male behavior, if seen as
an expression of both men's inner femininity and their search
for the mother or the matriarchal, is trying to explain an exclusively masculine behavior in feminine terms. This con-
fuses three independent variables in sexual identity: sex role,
sex orientation, and gender. Kinsey's work on sexual orientation as a fluid phenomena suggests we cannot overlook the
father's influence in male homosexuality, since the negative
father as absent, disappointing, or insensitive may lead to an
obsessive identification with masculinity and its archetypal
roots. Androgyny, as it comes into Jung's alchemical writings, suggests that homosexuality may enact the archetype of
the androgyne as a symbol of wholeness, and that self-gay sex
could be one form of the *coniunctio*, as an incomplete de-
tachment from the original archetype of the hermaphrodite,
or an unbroken state of non-differentiation—a bisexual response. An androgynous self could be just taking refuge in a
primal symbiosis as defense against individual identity and
feelings; or, it could be an embodiment of integration, a constant inner self that could respond either to men or women
sexually without threat to one's core self or soul. In general,
Jungian analysts have tended to abandon theoretical presup-
position in treating male homosexuality, and have concen-
trated on integrating the patient's unconscious aspects to en-
courage ideals and cultural/spiritual development.

In the myth of Apollo and Admetus, we encounter an archetype of male-to-male Eros. Lopez-Pedraza remarks on
patterns of male-to-male Eros as "falling in love with another man's fantasy" (1977, 79). Hermes' love for the nymph
of mortal King Dryops results in the birth of Pan, whose sexuality and wildness is the fruit of male-to-male Eros in the
myth in an hermetic way. Lopez-Pedraza emphasizes the importance of finding Pan's image in analyzing gay men:

> My attempt has been to discuss the image from the view-
> point of an archetypal psychology and particularly to stress
> the fact that Pan's birth was made possible by two men
> loving each other through a nymph. The insight that Pan is
> concerned with the psychotherapy of the body can open a

door for a psychotherapeutic approach to the pathologies attributed to him. It can offer, also, a psychotherapeutic approach to the analytical situation in which the patient's homosexuality appears center stage. Instead of a homosexuality with no psychological body, this approach could provide that same homosexuality with the body psychology of Pan, son of Hermes. (Lopez-Pedraza 1976, 189)

Mitch Walker of the San Francisco gay community believes that there is for men a soul figure with the erotic and spiritual power of one's anima who is not a shadow but a double, but not just a symbol of self or ego. In the Babylonian creation myth, Gilgamesh, who is half-God and half-man, has as an ideal comrade, Enkidu. Enkidu is Gilgamesh's second self, his own reflection. Robert Hopcke writes, "If anything, Enkidu functions as the anima might for Gilgamesh—appearing in Gilgamesh's dreams as helper and guide, beautiful and enchanting in his wildness, a figure with its own mind and personality and yet one that deeply embodies Gilgamesh's own inner self—and yet it is not the anima, as Jung intended the concept, since the double appears to be of the same sex" (1989, 117).

John Beebe believes that when anima is truly a soul figure as archetype, it may be either male or female serving the *function* of anima proscribed by Jung but not always in cross-gender images. Hopcke agrees:

[H]omo-Eros, whether enacted or simply fantasized, is not always an example of immaturity or a misunderstanding but rather at times an expression of the soul's inherent oneness with itself, a connection not to an Other in a *coniunctio* of male-female, but rather a lived psychological Self-expression embodied in a man's love for masculinity, outwardly and inwardly. . . . If it is this *coniunctio* that one feels, then the symbolic inward expression of it can only have a homosexual form and can only be embodied in the male anima or the female animus. Mitch Walker's ideal double, friend, companion, comrade, brother/sister and lover . . . (1989, 120)

Eugene Monick defends homosexuality from pathology (1987). In the clearest statement within the Jungian literature, he agrees with the Danish psychoanalyst Thorkel Van-gaard that every male has some capacity for homosexual interest. Monick sees three differing pressures on men to become homosexual: the homosexual radical inherent in every man, the emergency of eroticism based on this need, and then the actual acting out of homosexual desire in sexual behavior.

I agree with Hopcke, who understands very well that a description of homosexuality involves a "kaleidoscope of patterns, urges, impulses, fantasies, and purposes to homosexuality"(1989, 1992) that interweave between three archetypes: the masculine, the feminine, and the androgyne. I am also as concerned as Hopcke is, in analyzing homosexuals, that the individuation of gays takes place in a pressured psychosocial context that includes continuing political homophobia resulting from the patriarchal, one-sided, masculine type concerned with dominant control, and the oppression of positive femininity and non-macho masculinity. Contact with the real inner and outer facts of homosexuals' lives today is what analysts must attain if they are to assist the individuation of gay patients in a reliable and sufficient way. I want to proceed, therefore, with an informal case description of a patient, which I hope will help further the reader's comprehension of the complexity of gay orientation.

Tim's Case

Tim was born into a working-class family. His father was employed in a small factory in a moderately skilled job; his mother had left high school to take any available clerking work. Tim is the only homosexual I have worked with who knew even before he entered primary school, at five years of age, that he "wanted" only males in his life. His memory of the earliest time of his infancy never came through in analysis. It was truly blacked out. There had been no definite physical or psychological abuse, but he did experience an Oedipal rivalry, as the younger of two sons, that engendered his powerful rejection of his father and his sympathy with his mother. If Tim ever actually contacted or loved the feminine (as principle), it was only contained by his mother and then only when he was very young. By the time he reached the age of seven, only the male half of the human population was consciously any longer of interest to Tim: no female was ever again to be deeply experienced as important, or to be noticed beyond a fleeting moment of the barest civility. Tim was living an extremely radical homosexual fundamentalism.

Tim was thirty when he came into therapy, ostensibly because he had broken off with his first long-term partner, an ambitious but not very gifted young actor who was never to have a career. Tim had been initiated to active sexuality by his male teachers at a boarding school to which he had won a scholarship. He achieved an excellent academic career in order to be upwardly mobile, having no money and feeling shame for his family background. By the time he entered university, he had known an incredible number of male sexual partners. Yet Tim's memory dimmed until well into analysis as to the numbers and kinds of homosexual acts he had performed. Later, with his doctors, after he was diagnosed as HIV-positive, he estimated he had known 1,200 different sex partners before he reached age thirty. He had experimented with every known gay sexual act, working as a male prostitute one summer "just to see how this felt." After leaving university, Tim gradually achieved a brilliant business career, and through earning power climbed socially to a higher echelon of homosexual society. He rarely even took a meal with a woman or attended mixed parties. but only socialized with men. Extremes were Tim's way of life.

Tim entered the Eastern Orthodox Christian Church in his late teens and there found a place to project his more feeling emotions. He identified more with the crucified Christ than with a resurrected One, and this worried me once his HIV diagnosis was established. The genuine suffering this brought into Tim's analytical work was so profoundly authentic that several changes came over him. He tried to be faithful to a new, long-term lover with more effort than he had ever before expended. Although Tim couldn't successfully refrain from promiscuity in spite of his efforts, he seemed to experience a deeper empathy for others in a new and Christian way. Nevertheless, ruthlessness that constantly overwhelmed his more outgoing impulses ultimately seemed to strangle Tim's impulses. This ruthlessness always defeated a growth in character. Tim's behavior retained a controlling, obsessive, and self-centered core as *modus vivendi*. In the "theatre" of England's class consciousness and love for acting out extremes, Tim found an admiring circle always ready to support his behavior which, in analysis, gave him concern.

Obsession has always been very difficult to transform analytically. I released hope early on in the work for a total eradication of this pathology in my patient. However, I always remained alert for any opportunity to work with obsessions creatively, and certain behavior patterns related to this in Tim did alter, loosen, and partly integrate. An illustration of obsessional control in Tim arrived concerning the arrangements of care for his mother, who died after a series of strokes. Tim fell into a rivalry in this situation, asserting unconscious control, insisting on taking over all of the private nursing arrangements, moving his mother to a strange city, and almost controlling the visits of his father and older brother as well. Here was Oedipal rivalry acted out yet again under the guise of a well-meant financial and "rational" generosity. But Tim was never able to imagine, as many very ambitious worldly people cannot, that others may have had feelings about how his mother should spend her last days.

Ultimately, I believe that Tim was locked into a radicalized ego that did not have permeable boundaries to the wider unconscious knowledge in the self. He rarely could recall dreams over several years, suggesting support for this idea. This exaggerated ego split from the deeper unconscious resonance of self was Tim's abnormality, one that his social and educational condition did not entirely explain. His powerful Oedipal complex, with which we worked analytically, would not entirely explain this extreme.

Recently I wrote theoretically about self, the immune system, and aspects of physiological/psychological healing in this way, and I refer the reader to the appendix to this volume for a detailed discussion. In Tim's case, as his health began to waver within the HIV-positive condition and became full-blown AIDS, I retained some hope that further psychological consciousness might be enabled in analysis, through the therapeutic relationship that helped Tim's total situation. I hoped for either a remission, which is rare, or for a situation in which an aided and assisted illness allowed us to work through Tim's positive transference to me, which work has actually increased his positive transferences to others close to his personal life.

Tim has courage. This trait will need continuing inner transformation within him and within my own counter-transference to him as patient. For a therapist, there is always much to learn from each patient. Moving together in the valley of the shadow of death requires courage both in patient and in analyst. A further differentiation and integration can result in both psyches.

I have not tried to present Tim's case in clinical detail, but I have chosen to describe a few aspects of his life. The atmosphere around this material in its diversity would suggest that almost all the assertions of this chapter on homosexuality may be experienced by a single individual who lives a radically gay fundamentalist life. In my clinical practice it has become apparent to me that homosexuality is natural, but it appears to be more a matter of nurture than it is comprised of sufficiently proven genetic components. As a way of life for men, its prevalence is so widespread that its sociology has become more of an issue than trying to find a reductive cause for its complex induction into individuals' lives. Both the Freudian and Jungian contributions have relevance, but a further depth of perception is needed by the analytic profession if the profession is to grow in its understanding of same-gender love and passion in sexual expressions. Sexuality is always "more" than it appears to be, never "less."

III

Heterosexuality and Feeling

Only the eagle may look into the sun.

Russian Proverb

HETEROSEXUALS MAKE ONE assumption that is incorrect; they assume, if heterosexual, it means one is "like" other heterosexuals in sexual life. No one analyzing the sexual histories of male heterosexuals could agree. One overwhelming fact emerges in case histories; there is such a wide range of behavioral variation in actual heterosexual experience that each person's sexuality must be considered for its own uniqueness. The only thing male heterosexuals probably have in common is that they penetrate a woman's body by preference. Otherwise, their foreplay, time in penetration of orifices other than the vagina, regularity or otherwise of sexual coitus, after-sex behavior, place of sexual acts, and numbers of partners vary so enormously as to make classification difficult.

Some men describe the number of different women seduced as their "scoring." Quality of the sexual experiences seems less memorable or important for some than variety and excitement. Other men in monogamous marriages describe how loyalty, familiarity, and commitment enhance their sexual pleasure by placing it into a more spiritual place in psyche. To these men, feelings of union, completion, and wholeness dominate the discussion as more important than variety of seduction. Other men suffer by being caught between feelings of loyalty and gratitude to a wife, and temptations beyond their control to seduce other women in "affairs" which overwhelm them. Confused guilt results very often, leading to destructive feelings both towards themselves and their partners, and requiring the greatest analytical tact from psychotherapists. These men seek therapy, but then may run away from their therapy before resolution and integration is achieved psychologically. Men still have a curious lack of awareness within their early sexual lives, however much it may consume them. In fact, active males can reveal a kind of sexual ignorance that is surprising.

Men are confused about which physical features in themselves most attract women sexually. An alarming study in New York City, which I will quote, suggests that men do not understand what most physically attracts women (*Village Voice* 1975). Men imagine, in this research study, that women most admire a muscular chest and shoulders. But actually, small buttocks in men was voted by women to be most "sexy." Men thought secondly that muscular arms would be next more attractive, but women voted for slimness. Thirdly, men supposed large genitals to be next important. However, women rated a flat stomach in third place. In fourth rank, men voted for tallness as a sexual virtue; women ranked beautiful eyes in fourth place. And so on— there was no agreement between the sexes in ranking what is sexually attractive to women in men's physiques. How unconscious can men and women be concerning the primal scene as physical?

In a recent University of California study, men rated physical attractiveness as the most important of ten factors in evaluating desirable attributes in a female partner, with erotic ability, affectional ability, and social ability coming next in this order (Centeres 1972). Women tended to mention character, honesty, sincerity, and warmth before they cited a man's physical attractiveness as essential to the primal scene. At the University of Illinois, research has shown that men can be classified according to which part of the female anatomy most preoccupies their sexual images; breasts, bottoms, and legs were considered (Wiggens et al. 1968). For example, men who prefer very large breasts tend to be smokers, sportsmen, readers of pornography, and are frequent daters. Men who prefer small breasts tend to be non-drinkers, religious, depressed, and submissive. A preference for large bottoms goes with obsessional men, the passive, the guilt-prone, and those with a need for order. Small bottoms are preferred by the persevering and the non-sporting. Large legs are liked by non-drinking men, the submissive, the self-abasing, and the socially inhibited. Small legs attract extroverts, exhibitionists, the nurturing male, and the sociable male.

Generally women list achievement, leadership, and occupational and economic ability as what they need from men more than their degree of sexual attractiveness. It would behoove women to notice their own power gratification through these projected achievement needs, which their partnering men must contain over and above male attractiveness. This supports my idea that many women have lived out their power needs vicariously through their men. In fairness, it is also biologically true that human males respond more to visual female invitation signals than to non-visual signals. Women respond less to male visual signals than vice versa. Here we are partly dealing with primate evolutionary trends which are driving the sexes to have different needs in one another, and which restrict conscious knowledge of how the other sex really is attracted. In this age of sexual promiscuity and confusion, the facts contained in these sexual studies may or may not come as a surprise to the reader.

With the increased availability of video pornography, a concern with sexual athleticism, separated from the feeling atmosphere around the sexual act, has swept across the world since the 1950s. At the height of this recent mania, I heard a London woman who was husband-hunting say, "I will sleep with anyone who wants me, but if a man has even one premature ejaculation, that man is crossed off my list of a potential husband immediately." I am not surprised that such a woman pushes men towards becoming hostile and self-protective, in response to this kind of hysterical reaction to occasional sexual disappointment. One man, in dealing with this woman, had a vasectomy, as he had had children of his own and did not want more with a woman who wanted control and manipulation of sex with only her own needs in mind. Sexual relationship is a two-way affair.

On the other hand, ever since Adam found Eve without and within, there is a sense in which men have had a confused standard in their conduct toward women. A story about Sir Thomas Beecham, that sharp-tongued orchestral conductor, illustrates what I mean. Asked whether it was true that he did not like to have women in the orchestra, Sir Thomas said, "Well, I'm very fond of women, but in an orchestra, if they're not good-looking—and often they're not and they always look worse if they're blowing—it puts me off, while if they're good-looking it puts me off a damn sight more" (Alkins and Newman 1978). So here is a man saying that he cannot help having a physical response to women, one way or another, and that this clouds the issue of the woman's musicality, that she is more seen than heard even in an orchestra. That is surely male chauvinism and is unacceptable, in that it is denying a woman's talents in the place of work itself.

Our Judeo-Christian culture has much to answer for concerning male chauvinism, for it traditionally undervalued the feminine by refusing to worship any God but a male God, Yahweh, the so-called "jealous" God who would have no other Gods before himself: he didn't even mention the possibility of having a female consort, much less a liberated feminist who might share the power of Godhead equally. Adam and Eve, in one version of the Bible's creation myth (Gen. 2), has Eve fashioned from Adam's rib to be a helpmate to him. We all know what feminists rightly think of this version where primacy of the male tried to get itself established. In Genesis 1, there is another version of the Adam and Eve myth in which they are created together: "so God created man in His own image, in the image of God created He him; male and female created He them" (Gen. 1:27–28). Kabbalah scholars point out that earlier, in Genesis 1:26, the Hebrew version proclaims, "And Elohim said, let Us make man"—Elohim as both male and female.

Elohim wasn't alone. In the ancient pyramid texts of Egypt, the ultimate but hidden godhead, Atum, was androgynous in its aboriginal form as the arbiter of destiny—and was referred to as "that great he/she" in 2800 B.C. But this androgyny of God as a concept was already obscured by the time the Hebrew Bible was codified during the 6th century B.C. By that time, the Hebrews had wandered as nomads from the Syrian desert to Canaan, and had overthrown several city-states as they did their walk-abouts and ride-abouts; they enthroned male aggression as Yahweh, Lord of a patriarchal society, a very masculine and very angry Father-God.

Babylonians meanwhile retained a concept of a primal androgyny, and this theme is also found in the Midrash where it is said, "Adam and Eve were made back to back and were joined at the shoulders. Then God divided them with an axe stroke, cutting them in two." Mircea Eliade thought that spiritual perfection consisted in rediscovering within oneself this androgynous nature. We do know that in alchemy one of the names of the philosopher's stone was the "double being," or the hermetic androgyne. June Singer points out to us that the opus of alchemical work would be to refine and to differentiate this primal androgyny into a new consciousness, a new androgyny:

> On the one side is the female androgyne, a woman whose predominantly feminine humanity is able to bear its fruit by reason of continuous fertilization from her animus. On the other side is the male androgyne, a masculine person, who has found a place of incubation for the seeds of his creativity, in the dark moist depths of his own soul. (Singer 1976)

Jung has ascribed a name to the inner figure of woman that is held by a man; this is named "anima." The psychic image of the figure of man at work in a woman's psyche is named "animus." They are not just contrasexual counterparts of maleness and femaleness, but act as guides of the soul or as *psychopompi*. Jung saw these soul-images, which function from within the unconscious psyche, as "not-I." In a man, this not-I corresponds to a soul or spirit seen as feminine in principle. In a woman, the not-I, or animus, corresponds to a masculine Logos that is unconsciously used within a woman's psyche. Both anima and animus are felt to be *"a priori* elements of moods, reactions, impulses in man; of commitments, beliefs, inspirations in a woman—and for both something that prompts one to take cognizance of whatever is spontaneous and meaningful in psychic life" (Samuels et al. 1986).

The archetypal animus force in women and the anima force in men seem to be at their most omnipotent and rather infantile period of early flowering in recent times. In a small London book shop, I recently found 130 books on the shelves about feminist emancipation and only four books about men. Men, beware of this imbalance of information and of feeling about your gender, your brothers. The animus is shouting out—the anima is too still. Some women today announce that men are not important to them. Many women furthermore expect to be respected for this attitude, if not envied and admired for it. Independence "is all," and in the process of achieving it, a woman may delude herself that she actually is both man and woman like the back-to-back Adam and Eve before God divided the two parts.

Vive la différence . . . may I caricature this whole situation just to make a point? A woman decides to reject men but wants a child. She goes along to the local sperm bank where she can arrange a conception by a computer date with a sperm sample which is anonymous to her (but not to the computer programmer, please note). She is then impregnated by artificial insemination in a laboratory. My extreme woman sees a male-dominated society as "out there" and she tends to ignore the negative aspects of her inner animus which is quite marauding and unrelated if not domineering. She is being all the things she hates in men.

The anima in men has also fallen behind its ideal development and is just as dangerous in its regressive infantilism. The stereotype of British men in high places, or at least in forward ones, gives an impression of obedient schoolboys, their anima caught up in a strange Oedipal dance with their Victorian matriarch, their mothers. These men are in an unconscious search for their own fathers, who so often were rarely present except for a few hours on school visiting days. Have you ever noted the abandoned faces of public school boys when family visiting hours are over? All this leaves a development of an unconscious dependency upon mother. Jung has pointed out that this is not a good idea for independent masculine development after middle teen-age.

Many men make strong projections that hook onto "power-women." Then men reincorporate these images within—a very little Eros is actually incorporated and the man's personality becomes expressed as a rather edgy, battle-axed expression of uncertain Logos, a kind of inner, loud adolescent, a kind of anorexic anima with an under-nourished feeling to it. This anima is rejecting, thin-on-the-ground, weak, deferent, and has a hostile persona or outer effect. With all of these insufficiently balanced personalities around, it can be quite difficult to admire or easily get on with one's brothers and sisters in this era of inner and outer masculine/feminine conflict in the collective. But I would like to hope that in spite of evidence to the contrary, the contrasexual inner images—the animus in women and the anima in men—so long historically restricted from fuller expression and therefore volatile and power-driven, may, in time, in both men and women become inner images that are slightly less mysterious. They need to be more easily grasped and balanced by both sexes in new forms of consciousness. This integration of the animus and anima would be one of the great dreams of the Aquarian Age.

I believe the deepest contemporary problem for women with men is one concerning the underdeveloped feeling function in many men. Men communicate very little about their real feelings, once they enter a tough, competitive world of achievement in work. They tend to exhaust themselves, using thinking, sensation and intuition in the game of economic survival. When they meet their women after a working day, they often cannot feel their way into her working or domestic problems. Men don't particularly want to have to discipline their children for the latters' daily misdemeanors, because they want positive relationships—often in the form of play, helpful fathering, and teaching about the real world outside the domestic scene. There is a danger if wives, with or without careers, become less and less compassionate to the difficulties of outer-world achievement their husbands actually experience, then men will turn away from marriage to any liaison that brings them reassurance, understanding, relaxation, and profound acceptance of themselves as they are.

The Greek idea of the hero, or today's antihero, may have done much to put men into relationship problems, perhaps more than any other set of myths. How many men, in today's socioeconomic climate of dog-eat-dog competition, can achieve something heroic in the eyes of women? I am not suggesting that male heroes don't exist among us, but they are often publicly unknown and bear little, if any, resemblance to those larger-than-life Greek heroes.

Mothers and wives push men on to assimilate and express their own feminine ruthlessness, rather than to simply give support to the man's realistic natural ambition. This pressure can destroy a man's true humanity, often the price for so-called heroic achievement. The psychic gun at a man's back is his wife's withholding of conjugal sexual activity, if he fails either in the marketplace or in relation to her images of the masculine. A drug-ridden pop world culture suggests that to de-struct in style before screaming lights, screaming microphones, screaming electric guitars, and screaming fans is the latest song from the hill of Calvary for the male hero. To con-struct maleness seems further from the collective grasp than one cares to realize.

How could men find more feeling in themselves? Part of a true feeling function deals with an ongoing constructive differentiation in its evaluation of all experience. But men are often driven to functioning for the sake of function alone. I suggest that in men, feeling has often been restricted to the Latin root meaning of function—*functor*—which means to perform. Men "perform" their feelings rather than enjoy the critical differentiation of feeling which is a deeper capacity. But *functus*, in Latin, is associated with enjoyment as is the Sanskrit root of functioning—*bhuhj*—which refers to enjoying. The feeling function should be a man's value judgment within an enjoyable intentionality.

Let us look at formulations about the feeling function. Here is one of Jung's, from volume 6 of his *Collected Works*:

[F]eeling is a kind of judgment, differing from intellectual judgment in that its aim is not to establish conceptual relations but to set up a subjective criterion of acceptance or rejection. The valuation by feeling extends to every content of consciousness, of whatever kind it may be. When the intensity of feeling increases, it turns into an affect, a feeling-state accompanied by marked bodily innervations. (Jung 1971, par. 725)

Here is another formulation about feeling by James Hillman:

[S]o much is feeling the problem of the times that one could preposterously assert that the whole field of psychotherapy resulted from inadequacies of the feeling function. Our personal feeling problems are partly the result of the ages of suppression, which have by no means been lifted by the confused enthusiasms of the eighteenth century or by the pornographic delights of the mid-twentieth. Our feeling problems are collective problems, and we need new fantasies for them. To deal with them only directly, with a new doctrine of feeling and a revolution in its name, is not enough. The shibboleths of the age are "connect," "relate," "be human," "be sincere," "feel," . . . but how? And what do these slogans mean? (Hillman and von Franz, 1971)

It is true that Jung did much to resurrect a concept of feeling and separate it from just any affectivity. All of Jung's principal conceptual ideas, such as archetype, introversion, self, shadow, and synchronicity, are experiences which contain feeling. All complexes are feeling-toned. Self-realization, in part, is a feeling realization. We learn to feel our thoughts and to sense our intuitions.

Anima and Eros in men should not be merged carelessly with Jung's concept of feeling. Anima, as the feminine aspect of the masculine psyche, has feminine imagery. But Eros has masculine imagery: Adonis, Cupid, Jesus, Krishna, Buddha, Mohammed, etc. The Eros principle, in men who contain it, is active and aimed. It is not passive. Feeling as a function operates in a tighter space and time situation than do anima or Eros. A person's feeling may manifest Eros and be archetypally rooted there, but it functions to evaluate a situation, a person, a moment, an object, an alternative, or even its own feeling-tone. Feeling imparts value in connecting a subject to an object. It is the function of relationship. It concerns the reason of the heart, the appreciation of social and ethnic values, of taste, of ethical forms, of personal timing and tact, of religious instincts, of sexual choices, and of the nature of creativity.

How could men instigate a feeling function that would suit today's more emancipated women? Firstly, while the anima may stimulate the feeling function, it is never the equivalent of feeling. Anima remains the spiritual life principle, and in men may have been projected onto mythical feminine figures such as Aphrodite, Ariadne, Artemis, or Persephone. These images strike me as over-evaluations, when a feeling evaluation might use a more average contemporary woman as a sufficient anima projection: that is, Mr. Everyman might constellate a feeling image of Miss Everywoman rather than needing a goddess to reveal the feminine. If Jungians get stuck on the larger-than-life figures of Greek myths as their breath of life, I can only feel that will inflate them. And, indeed, it often has! Where man's feeling function is weak, the anima will take more feeling-tone to itself, in compensation, as it receives and contains the activation of unconscious events. The danger of archetypal takeover is thus a collective threat to men unless they get in touch with, and use, their feeling function. And how grateful women would be for that development.

As the Greek images of gods and goddesses sometimes fail to suit men's desire to be whole and to contain successfully the feminine in their inner life, I have turned to the masculine images of ancient Egypt for inspiration in being male. In Barbara Hannah's book, *Active Imagination* (1981), she discusses a manuscript by an Egyptian man from a text four thousand years old. I wish to discuss this material as to man's masculine survival and as an echo of some of the ideas we have considered. An Egyptologist, Helmut Jacobsohn, provided the background study concerning this "world-weary man," as the Egyptian named himself, whose writings were found on a papyrus from about 2200 B.C. At that time the Egyptians believed that true existence only occurs after a man's death. Egypt was undergoing the breakup of the Old Kingdom, which reminds one of modern revolution now. The religious priests were murdered, the rich exterminated, and almost every prince wanted to be Pharoah.

The "world-weary man" was experiencing psychological shock and turned to his *Ba*, or soul, in dialogue. His *Ba* was an image of a psychic being which connected a man to the incarnation of the god, Osiris. The *Ba* was depicted in hieroglyphics as a human-headed bird hovering over the mummy in a man's tomb. As the world-weary man needed Osiris, the god of survival and a representative of man's autonomous unconscious, that man dared cry out to his *Ba* while still mortal, against the dogma of his time which had relegated dialogue with the Spirit to the post-mortal state.

The Sun God, Re, father of Osiris, was another masculine god of incomparable importance to masculine Logos in Egypt. In the tradition of Egypto-Chaldean star-worship, the Sun was the idea of solar Logos and became an archetype of beauty and of being itself. The legend of Mithras goes back 200 years before the Christian myth and was introduced to Rome by 67 B.C. The legend had Mithras born on December 25 in a cave next to a sacred tree by a stream. This marked the winter solstice of the ancient world, which today in Europe is on December 21, after which the sun is "reborn." In general, the sun is a perfectly good analogue to Christ; the Church even identifies Him with the sun in Malachi 4:2: "But unto you that fear my name shall the Sun of righteousness arise with healing in his wings." Let us visualize the Sun God Re rising as a scarab at sunrise; the Sun God then flies upward as a hawk (a reference to man's first half of life in his ego development); then the Sun God turns every hour of the day into a symbol (a reference to deepening connections at midlife). Then, as the sun sets, the Crocodile God called Sobek appears. At midnight (or in the unconscious) the Crocodile God puts together the pieces of the victims he has eaten during the day. This resurrection improves the quality of the devoured. This reminds one of the integrated adjustments needed by men in the second half of life, as the totality of the mature self relativizes the ego into a new integration and function.

Whatever may prevent the light of the sun from passing through the unconscious, guided by the *Ba* Spirit, is the greatest threat to self-development an ancient Egyptian could experience. When men first look into their unconscious, perhaps through depression, it seems grey. Barbara

Hannah remarks that Jung used to say, "all cats are grey in the dark." In Jungian language, the *Ba* Spirit would be a man's anima, which negotiates between our consciousness and the self as one's totality. The Egyptian religions of four thousand years ago clearly formulate that a man is responsible for knowing that a self has existence within him. If the anima is weak, men should consider what it is being projected and modeled. In addition to a possible splitting, splintering, and contamination by those Greek goddesses, men struggle with projections onto others' wives, mistresses, and the never-ending stream of Lolitas—these nubile, adolescent, hysterical sex "kittens." Men also struggle with weak male prototypes and with a phallic-style arrogance in some women who are overcome with animus-ridden power demons. It is refreshing to begin to see men express anger directly toward those to whom they feel that anger, whatever their gender. The image of the ideal man as "steady" has been overdone in Britain, and the gentleman (of a time almost gone by) has no one for whom to fling down his coat to assist crossing the mud puddle. His lady has already waded through the mud, splashing the gentleman liberally as she goes racing ahead, her psychic energy charging all boundaries with an animus-takeover bid.

Reactively, a vicious cycle may develop as a man's mirroring anima creates its own malignant children, the nuclear atomic missile. All the Egyptians needed to show masculine strength and power was an obelisk, not an atomic missile! We need as men to lead our anima to an integrating with the *Ba* Spirit of old which could then deal directly with Osiris, the male god of regeneration and survival. This has not collectively happened and men have failed to rule the world wisely. Greed and power have overwhelmed men's better humanitarian judgments.

Man is the predator of man. He has also devastated his environment and its surrounding atmosphere in many parts of the world. When man realizes that to learn about what is different from himself, he must do it through the feminine in women, his own anima, and his feeling values, then he will again, by contrast, understand the Sun God Re, that truly masculine deity from Egypt. Jung wrote, "Masculinity is knowing what one wants and doing what is necessary to achieve it." But this is a one-sided definition. Jung also was aware of that and wrote that if a man wants to be a god, he is in danger of forgetting that he is "only the stable in which the god is born." If men live out their life as completely as possible, to the bitter or not-so-bitter end, this entails not only a conflict with the world and the flesh, but an acceptance of suffering and a certain re-formation in the way one sees one's own individual life.

The best evocation I ever found about the masculine was written by a woman in the personal column advertisements in a London newspaper, "Dear Henry, being with you last weekend and always is like being with the sun! Love, Elsie."

IV

Fathering

Truth is much stranger than fiction.

Old Proverb

IN JUNG'S PAPER, "The significance of the father in the destiny of the individual," he discussed the overwhelming power of the parents' image in a child's life:

> Freud has pointed out that the emotional relationship of the child to the parents, and particularly to the father, is of decisive significance in regard to the content of any later neurosis. This is indeed the infantile channel along which the libido flows back when it encounters any obstacles in later years, thus reactivating the long forgotten psychic contents of childhood. . . . If the patient is a neurotic, he reverts back to the childhood relationships he has never quite forsaken, and to which the normal person is fettered by more than one chain—the relationship to father and mother. . . . The source of the infantile disturbance of adaptation is naturally the emotional relation to the parents. . . . The neurosis sets in the moment the libido is withdrawn from the infantile relationship, and for the first time comes a bit nearer to an individually determined

> goal. . . . The power which shapes the life of the psyche has
> the character of an anonymous personality. . . . The
> parental imago is possessed of quite extraordinary power; it
> influences the psychic life of the child enormously. (Jung
> 1909, par. 693)

The "missing father" is a psychological and actual fact typical of our time in society. Britain has the highest divorce
rate in Europe, where for young children the custody is almost always given to mothers under the law; effectively the
child loses the father to a considerable extent. Every five
years, about one million children face this separation from
father in home life. But fathers who are at home are often
experienced as largely unavailable. The father seems ineffec-
tive or obliterated by a dominating wife, from whom he does
not help a son to extricate himself.

Archetypally, a projected image is built up on an actual
father or a substitute father from the beginning, very clearly
so in babies from the fourth month. Later, fantasy figures or
power figures may be substituted from media images. What
sons seem to be seeking from father figures is some kind of
psychological alliance, even a tenuous one, as a part of a support system. Samuels points out that "the image of the elder
telling all he knows to the younger is a compelling one"
(1985, 33). The father in this is a spiritual force, a force of
conscience. Strength in the father gives a role model and
pushes the son to turn incestuous libido centered on mother
towards social and cultural ideals of achievement or influence in the outer world. Internal images needed by some
from their fathers touch on modes and qualities of behavior
involving courage, self-control in emergency, forceful
decision-making, and leadership.

Where a father holds to a preformed and unconscious
identification with the father archetype, a dangerous situation develops in a son imitating this (unconsciously). The
boy will incorporate his father's unconsciousness about fathering from outside, but has little conscious sonship at first
within himself to balance this effect. He is then au-
tonomously overcome, as is his father, with psychotic tendencies in the interrelationship.

Father and the Oedipal Myth

I want to consider the instability of fatherhood as it grew out of the Oedipal myth. For generations, storytellers have molded the Oedipal myth into an engaging mixture of archetype and myth, legend and fairytale. I am indebted to a London analyst, Dr. Karl Figlio, for a new interpretation of the Oedipal story as it affects our conceptualization of the father (Figlio 1985). Many, but not all of the ideas to follow are inspired by Dr. Figlio. Firstly, let us review the bare bones of the Oedipus story: Oedipus was the son of Laius, King of Thebes, and of Queen Jocasta. His father, having learned from an oracle that he was doomed to perish by the hands of his own son, exposed Oedipus on a mountainside, immediately after his birth, with his feet pierced and tied together. The child was found by a shepherd, who took him to the childless King and Queen of Corinth, who brought up Oedipus as their own son.

In his youth, Oedipus was told by the Oracle at Delphi that he would kill his father and marry his mother, and, horrified, he resolved never to return to Corinth. Ignorant of his true ancestry, he set out for Thebes and, on the road, encountered King Laius, whom he killed in a quarrel over the right-of-way. Here the theme of male competitive dominance over status, territory, and prestige comes forward as basic to men's murder of other men.

Near the city of Thebes, Oedipus answered the riddle of the Sphinx, then a plague to all travelers, and, for defeating this monstrous female winged lion, the Thebans made Oedipus their king. He married the widow Jocasta and so, unwittingly, fulfilled the prophecy of marrying his mother. In time, he learned he had killed his father and married his mother. This self-discovery caused him to blind himself before going into exile, where in a grove near Athens, the three Furies finally released Oedipus from an earthly existence. Jocasta, his mother and wife, hanged herself soon afterward.

So, in the classical Oedipus story, Oedipus kills his father and marries his mother. In psychoanalysis, Oedipus is said to kill his father in order to marry his mother. The change in emphasis introduces the father as a competitor, an intruder between the son and the mother. It makes the mother into the object of the son's love and the father into the envious rival of emerging youth. This envy of the father for the emerging youth of his sons is an important point to consider. The Oedipal conflict derives its intensity not from the strength of the father and his power to frustrate his son's desire, but from the regressive pull that levels the differences in experience between them and therefore threatens the hope for growth.

Another problem for the father is his insecurity about what the status of father is, compared to mother. Mothers physically bear their children; men do not. The male's lack of any physical experience, beyond copulation, in the bearing and delivering of the child leaves his psychic relationship rather at a primitive, almost magical level. Fatherhood seems to be more about the acceptance of paternity than the impregnation of the female. The father's acceptance of paternity demonstrates the emergence of the generations within history.

Whereas the woman can map her internal physical body-spaces through the conception of the child—that is, she can internally map her vagina because the entry of the penis helps her to do this, after which carrying the fetus helps her to map the womb as well—the male cannot. The creation of life is not particularly in his awareness; it is more possible for the female. The Oedipal myth expresses the uncertainty of fatherhood by regressively leveling the relationship between father and son. In fact, the Oedipal story tells us that there are psychological situations in which fatherhood, motherhood, and childhood may disappear as psychic realities, and that the unconscious may include that reality all the time.

The male relationships deteriorate between elder and younger males; the complementary admiration between father and son may turn to sadistic rivalry between them. When that happens, the father-son relationship deteriorates into sibling rivalry; the father is then no more the father than the son is in the Oedipal story. They both regress to one level. Then the envy of the mother becomes uncontrollable. Envy of the breast means biting it off; castrating father means symbolically biting off his penis. Mythically, one then might eat the children, because in fantasy that would lead to omnipotently self-creating ourselves without mother or father left to trouble anyone.

Where father is absent, weak, or unloving, and doesn't give a real prototype for sons to sense as a good way to be as a father, then this self-omnipotence and ego-centeredness is forced onto sons from within as compensation for the lack of a positive father image. Where fathers don't help educate their sons, there they regressively forget their sons psychologically; then—like Oedipus—a son will feel adopted and so returns to the real mother or to the envy of the mother. This is usually unconscious. The loss of the masculine father image leads to the loss of hope in their sons for self-emergence, for making their mark upon the world. This loss forces sons into a primitive, omnipotent, self-created (as opposed to parented) way of behavior, and leads to destructive envy, unconsciously, as the son fights to prevent fusion-with-mother and sexual desire for her. The son may lose his own desire to become a father, because it seems as if he had no father whom he could wish to be like. Fathering deteriorates around the Oedipal story, a myth that is still in our contemporary lives.

Father as the Wise Old Man Archetype

Uncertainty can also overwhelm the father in drawing upon the Jungian archetype of the Wise Old Man. Jung has written that "the Wise Old Man has a positive and a wicked aspect . . . just as the primitive medicine-man is a healer and helper and also the dreaded concocter of poisons" (Jung 1945, esp. par. 413–18). In general, the positive elements of the Wise Old Man archetype are aspects of wisdom, reflection, insight, cleverness, intuition, and good moral conduct. But if these are the upward turning, positive, and favorable elements, there are the downward turning, chthonic, and partly negative aspects in the images of the Wise Old Man archetype

as well—aspects which come forward in stories and fairy
tales again and again.

Jung points out that:

> [I]n one Balkan tale, the old man is handicapped by the loss
> of an eye. It has been gouged out by the Vili, a species of
> winged demon, and the hero is charged with the task of
> getting them to restore it to him. The old man has there-
> fore lost part of his eyesight—that is, his insight and en-
> lightenment—to the daemonic world of darkness; this
> handicap is reminiscent of the fate of Osiris, who lost an
> eye at the sight of a black pig (his wicked brother Set) or
> again of Wotan, who sacrificed his eye at the spring of
> Mimir. Characteristically enough, the animal ridden by
> the old man in our fairy tale is a goat, a sign that he him-
> self has a dark side. In a Siberian tale, he appears as a one-
> legged, one-handed and one-eyed greybeard who wakens a
> dead man with an iron staff. In the course of the story the
> latter, after being brought back to life several times, kills
> the old man by mistake, and thus throws away his good
> fortune. The story is entitled "The One-sided Old Man,"
> and in truth his handicap shows that he consists of one
> half only. The other half is invisible, but appears in the
> shape of a murderer who seeks the hero's life. Eventually
> the hero succeeds in killing his persistent murderer, but in
> the struggle he also kills the one-sided old man, so that the
> identity of the two victims is clearly revealed. It is thus
> possible that the old man is his opposite, a life-bringer as
> well as a death-dealer—"ad utrumque peritus" (skilled in
> both), as is said of Hermes. Naturally one thinks of Merlin,
> whose ambiguities move from good deeds to apparently
> loving evil for evil's sake when he behaves as the "wicked
> magician."

Jung quotes another tale that reveals the many-sided nature
of the Wise Old Man archetype:

> A king is looking for his sister who has been abducted
> by a stranger. His wanderings bring him to the hut of an
> old woman, who warns him against continuing his search.
> But a tree laden with fruit, ever receding before him, lures
> him away from the hut. When at last the tree comes to
> a halt, an old man climbs down from the branches. He

regales the king and takes him to a castle, where the sister is living with the old man as his wife. She tells her brother that the old man is a wicked spirit who will kill him. And sure enough, three days afterwards, the king vanishes without trace. His younger brother now takes up the search and kills the wicked spirit in the form of a dragon. A handsome young man is thereby released from the spell and forthwith marries the sister. The old man, appearing at first as a tree-numen, is obviously connected with the sister. He is a murderer. In an interpolated episode, he is accused of enchanting a whole city by turning it to iron, i.e. making it immovable, rigid and locked up. He also holds the king's sister captive and will not let her return to her relatives. This amounts to saying that the sister is animus-possessed. The old man is therefore to be regarded as her animus. But the manner in which the king is drawn into this possession, and the way he seeks for his sister, makes us think that she has an anima significance for her brother. The fateful archetype of the old man has accordingly taken possession of the king's anima—in other words, robbed him of the archetype of life which the anima personified—and forced him to go in search of the lost charm, the "treasure hard to attain," thus making him the mythical hero, the higher personality who is an expression of the self. Meanwhile, the old man acts the part of the villain and has to be forcibly removed, only to appear at the end as the husband of the sister-anima, or more properly as the bridegroom of the soul, who celebrates the sacred incest that symbolizes the rejuvenation and transformation of the old man, but hints at a secret inner relation of evil to good and vice versa. So in this story we see the archetype of the old man in the guise of an evil-doer caught up in all the twists and turns of an individuation process. (Jung 1945, 413–18)

In fathering, as soon as a man draws upon the sensing of an inner Wise Old Man image he at once can feel either like a dwarf or a giant in relation to his children. Jung discusses this surprising set of feelings in a passage concerning the difficulty of expressing proportional balances when an archetypal image overwhelms one—such as the Wise Old Man motif.

Man's sense of proportion, his rational conception of big and small, is distinctly anthropomorphic, and it loses its validity not only in the realm of physical phenomena but also in those parts of the collective unconscious beyond the range of the specifically human. The atman is "smaller than small and bigger than big," he is "the size of a thumb" yet he "encompasses the earth on every side and rules over the ten-finger space." And of the Cabiri, Goethe says, "little in length/ mighty in strength." In the same way, the archetype of the Wise Old man is quite tiny, almost imperceptible, and yet it possesses a fateful potency, as anyone can see when he gets down to fundamentals. The archetypes have this peculiarity in common with the atomic world, which is demonstrating before our eyes that the more deeply the investigator penetrates into the universe of microphysics the more devastating are the explosive forces he finds enchained there. That the greatest affects come from the smallest causes has become patently clear not only in physics but in the field of psychological research as well. How often in the critical moments of life everything hangs on what appears to be a mere nothing! (Jung 1945, par. 413–18)

Thus in fathering there has been a psychologically difficult role obscured by the ambiguities of the Wise Old Man archetype and the vagaries of the Oedipal unconsciousness. These may push a child too one-sidedly. In an age when the media assure us that more fathers are sexually abusing their daughters or sons than ever before, it is interesting that Jung's view was that the unconscious aim of incest fantasy was not an actual desire for intercourse with a parent, but a symbolic expression of a longing for the rebirth of oneself through contact with a kind of parental soil (Samuels 1989, 68). This kind of regression, when acted out physically, however, carries ramifications that are extremely dangerous, and may suggest children are the perpetrators of incestuous action as much as their fathers may be. Let me give two brief clinical examples from my practice: one of a daughter/father incest, and the other of a younger fatherless man seducing and being seduced by an older substitute father figure who was not known to be bisexual.

Joan's Case

Joan was the only daughter of a wealthy business man in London. She had been raised in foreign finishing schools where lesbianism was rampant. This was enhanced by the adolescent girls' separation from males, and compounded by general loneliness. Joan had longed for a first sexual affair with a man, but her restricted upper-class seclusion hadn't yet brought her a lover by the time she returned to the parental home for a holiday at eighteen.

Her parents had sexually separated some time before this visit, through an incompatibility which was not consciously known to Joan. Unconsciously, however, Joan, who was extremely attractive and had had every advantage money and leisure can add to a young woman's cosmetic and exercise regime towards luxuriant beauty, realized in retrospect that she had played her own seductive part in the incest that was to follow. Her father, drunk, found her glamorous image a replica of her mother's looks at the time he had married. In a confusion of feeling including both aggression and incestuous passion, he entered Joan's bedroom where she, both frightened and fascinated, had intercourse with her father— not, in her own view, entirely unwillingly. Joan always took partial responsibility for what had happened.

Joan spent the rest of her life in a split between blaming her father in her subsequent unhappy sexual affairs with younger men and her failed marriage later, *and* the realization that she had needed and partly preferred the image of her father in bed with her more than she had subsequent male sexual partners. Siding in retaliation, however, with her "discarded" mother, Joan regressed to a lifelong uroboric fusion to her mother, exaggeratedly identifying with her and worshipping her in her divorced state. To some extent, in almost taking over her father's protective role with her mother, Joan also symbolically lived out her phallic lesbian tendencies. She continued to her death at sixty-five to use her striking beauty to torment men and women whenever possible, according to her own self-judgment and self-avowal.

In doing this seductive torment, Joan denied the fact

that she had desperately needed closeness. She claimed, however, that the incestuous sex with her father had opened to her the actuality of love, which she then ritually transferred toward her mother through guilt. She felt she had been the ultimate whore with her father; however, the desire her father actually had created in her was initially denied. Had guilt been less present or had Joan sought therapeutic help much earlier than she did, perhaps the true importance of this incestuous one-night stand might have been transformed without retaliation into a further in-depth understanding of relationship to her father and subsequent happier heterosexuality.

It was Mahler (1971) who suggested that the father is the "awakener from sleep," and can sometimes act to protect a child from an overwhelmingly suffocating mother. Of course, Mahler was not suggesting the trauma of sexual incest as the way this should be expressed. Joan experienced tragedy in her sexual intercourse with her father, not only because it broke incest taboos *but because she said she enjoyed it in a passionate way.* Afterwards she couldn't find a way to recuperate from incest in a satisfactory way. It pulled the love/hate tensions within her towards men beyond that tautness with which normal psyche can satisfactorily function sexually. Although any court of law would have blamed her father for incest, his act may have been a desperate act of true love and even a potentially fathering act that neither our culture nor our collective degree of honesty can yet sustain outside the personal individual honesty that Joan brought into the analytical consulting room. By the time she came for help, both her father and her mother were dead.

Ned's Case

Ned, another former patient of my practice, had begun engaging in heterosexual coitus at age sixteen, soon after his father died. Having left school early, Ned had casual jobs and casual sexual liaisons, as he fled his poor English background and traveled widely on the Continent just after

World War II. His erotic consciousness had been entirely riveted to young women. During his travels he met a Dutchman who befriended him and found him work in Amsterdam. He had met the man's wife and daughters, and, consciously, had no inkling of the relationship that was building. Although Ned may have been aware that the Dutchman was fatherly towards him and had always wanted a son, he did not know that the man was an active bisexual.

The inevitable night came when, with the two traveling together for business, Ned shared a room with his fatherly friend. After heavy drinking, Ned was initiated into a variety of homosexual acts by his older friend, acts which Ned enjoyed but didn't later act out with anyone else. I refer to this episode as father/son incest because it had all of the *psychological* import of such for Ned and his friend. Ned had never known his biological father's penis, but he could know his substitute father's penis in erection, penetration, and oral succor, making up for less than enough fathering and maternal nurture throughout his experience up to that time.

A figure moving largely in the lower-class shadows of a conformist society, Ned was not established, not settled, not committed to anything; so, these sexual acts with a father-substitute were entered into passionately and also out of curiosity. In this situation, the friendship survived the "incestuous-style" homoerotic union, and Ned gently suggested his "father" look elsewhere for physical sex. However, Ned remained close to him and even grateful for the intimacy it had brought to their love and affection. Ned remained heterosexual entirely after this experience but was grateful for the insight into polymorphic and pluralistic relationship it gave him with friends and society generally nonsexually later on. The unity it gave him was that a fatherly man had given him love, but a love he did not pursue. Ned did not need to sexualize male relationship again, and married a young woman before long to, as he said, "settle down."

The incest danger is a precarious one. For some its scars can last a lifetime; for others it is a transformative influence quietly left behind as a part of exposure to passionate life itself. When it comes metaphorically into relationships, it is probably the degree of aggression subsumed with either father/son or father/daughter that decides both its inherent tragedy and degree of destructiveness. When it is sexually acted out, few children or adults are probably prepared for the degree of idealization: the overvaluation of admiration between the partners is an incestuous sexual act by a child with a father. These acts create enormous or overwhelming difficulties in recuperating from "forbidden" love or love beyond the conscious psyche's expectations. I have deliberately suggested in the case material cited that the child may need sometimes to seduce the father in a manner that suggests an unconscious wish for the direct experience of the father's penis at the "center" of the psychological act. Whether or not this is the return to the image of the parents in bed, in the child's mind, needs further evidence from research (see Samuels 1989, 123–42). My present opinion would be that it separates the child's image from the parents in bed forever, as opposed to fusing with it. Both conditions may contain destructive and overwhelming elements for psyche.

On the other hand, the generation of men who are now between twenty-five and forty-five years old are finding the courage to develop their anima function and their feeling function in relation to fathering in a normal and effective way. They also try to learn about Eros from their women friends and partners. Their development as father is striking; they attend their child's birth and share the difficult round-the-clock baby schedule of the first year. This suggests a comfortable relationship to their creative anima and a dynamic use of the feeling function and of Eros.

A growing number of men are retaining their wife's family name with their own, believing a woman's background should not be subsumed or erased under a man's family name. This approach is visible in many social classes of Europe. The Mountbatten-Windsor family use this form as a designation to be followed in Britain. It has been used in Switzerland for many years, and also in Spain. It brings an equality of family name into the secular-legal world and expresses the protection of individuality within union between man and woman. To a certain extent, a man is fathering his wife, too, in accepting her father's name as equal to his own father's name. This enlarges family concepts from the primal scene to the broader spirit of a clan. In fathering others, whether biologically or psychologically or both, a man steadies and fathers himself. He is pushed into influence upon the next generation, one of man's most responsible tasks. He learns much about his own Zeitgeist by measuring his capacities in nurturing (as father) against his peers. When he has unconsciously introjected his own father's lacks and strains in fathering, he must become conscious of the problem, or again inflict these aspects onto the next generation, unless he rids himself of these tendencies. In observing a man's psychological fathering one learns much about male selfhood in dynamic action and its reflection in society at large.

V

Bisexuality and the Father Archetype

All nature wears one universal Green.

Henry Fielding, *Tom Thumb*

PSYCHOHISTORY AND especially sexual history points to understanding essential connections between the archetype and the reaction of the individual. Male homosexuality is prepatriarchal, so that in it the masculine is not detached from the feminine. I would defend the idea that this can also be true for the female bisexual as well as for the male bisexual, on the basis that these persons have experienced an obvious gender boundary permeability psychologically, but have not experienced either the real father or the archetypal father image as fully constellated. To indicate the way that male bisexuality may develop, I want to trace the histories of two educated bisexual men, aged thirty-six and fifty, and discuss these cases as shedding light towards a continuing reevaluation of bisexuality.

Sergio's Case

Sergio, at thirty-six, was one of those men who appear to have almost everything: health, wealth, and a free sexual life. That was only a superficial appearance that Sergio himself brought into his first session, when he asked if his bisexual behavior could be outgrown. I explained that it could be analyzed and reassessed but that this impact might exert unpredictable pressures on the psyche, and that my task was to unravel his sexual experience so far. I further noted that it was not my role to have any prejudicial influence on his sexual choices in future, but since analysis had both a spiritual and an instinctual aspect, in time his own psyche might discover a greater "peace of mind" and might sexually settle in some less complicated and conflicted way than at present.

Working with Sergio, the only son of a wealthy Italian industrialist, was not easy. Because his father was constantly away for business reasons and his mother very socially driven, Sergio had been raised by servants and sent to private school by age nine. Parental contact occured largely on those rare occasions when the boy was wanted at the dinner table, or on holidays spent either in large rental mansions abroad or in separate suites in five-star hotels. The family staff were the persons who actually held, touched, or cuddled Sergio in his own memory of infancy, so it was established in analysis that his bisexual search for physical pleasure in his late teens partly represented both a search for mother and a search for father at first. Sexual curiosity ran high in his exclusive Catholic private school, and Sergio's first sexual contact was homosexual and pleasant. An older student initiated Sergio to this, but drifted away from the liaison and the following summer, at age eighteen, Sergio had intercourse with a girl of the same age he met on holiday in southern Italy. Unfortunately this experience scarred Sergio, who reached orgasm very quickly in his excitement. His partner was primitively angry—addressing him all sorts of pejoratives for coming too soon—and literally kicked him out of the bedroom. So negative a first heterosexual experience may have influenced Sergio's trust of women's sexual nature for some time.

At twenty, Sergio took up a longer-term homosexual partnership with a distinguished older doctor who had a fashionable Milan practice. Sergio lived at his family home outside Milan while taking a year free before entering university. He contrived to meet the doctor after lunch in a secret studio hideaway where they could be alone and unrecognized. This relationship was powerful, thoughtful, and caring, and swung Sergio's preference towards a mildly promiscuous homosexuality for the next ten years. Male partners never chided him for any sexual reason and the furtive closeness of this still secret life seemed sufficiently to hold his sexual needs. Sergio passed a basic but undistinguished degree course at university and took an office job in his father's administration department. He slowly worked his way up to a managerial post by age thirty.

There was now family social pressure on Sergio to marry. Several young women who dated him casually were genuinely attracted to him; then these women would move on when Sergio made no sexual advances by the third or fourth date. He seduced a gifted actress, with whom he had a brief but very important sexual fling. This went reasonably well, without passion but with considerable attraction, affection, and humor. Had this woman wanted marriage the possibility might have arisen, but she left for work in Hollywood and Sergio was left behind, heir to a financial fortune but alone. He was trapped into an office and a local society which bored him. He became increasingly isolated as his friends either married to have children or publicly declared themselves homosexual. Sergio felt uneasy socially and not entirely himself in either of these worlds. He disliked the gay world and avoided gay bars and gay night life. His childhood felt like a maze of lonely unloved agony, and we worked through a reconstruction of his first thirty years, a process that took three years of analytic sessions. This work enabled Sergio to begin to discover a nascent, emergent self.

At thirty-one Sergio had transferred to a London office of his family's business, where he felt freer of family and peer pressure. He was well liked in London, and after five years he came to work in analysis with me. Two homosexual affairs in England were now over. His transference at first projected me into a father substitute, then a brother substitute.

My countertransference corrected both attitudes, until I was simply an older heterosexual man who could be trusted. Sergio became able to trust me only very slowly as the intensity of his need to find trust made him idealize me, a situation I constantly defused so as to enable a sense of balanced equality in the analytic relationship to develop. Sergio wanted me to be his spiritual advisor, but I constantly referred him to the Catholic Church, as he was a Catholic of real religious feeling and I wanted several men to have influence upon his life in a positive sense. This included business friends. He tended to be disappointed in his contact with priests and business associates, although loyal to the Church in spirit and in letter.

Sergio's sexual activity abated as we worked more deeply through his father problem. We agreed on several things: first, that his curiosity about his father's sexual drive and men's sexual drive in general had led him to homosexual acts—as if to discover what maleness was and to reduce this to sexual acts separate from Sergio's sense of a wider cultural surrounding life; second, that his anger at his father's distance in Sergio's infancy may have led the boy towards heterosexual competition with his father, at first with distant fantasies of his mother as idealized, then bruised by awkward and unhappy sexual choices with young girls in his late teens. His actress partner had been healing as a true but temporary mistress. However, she was carried off by her talent into the media world, outside his family sense of what is appropriate within wealthy class mores. She lived in the asexual world of the film industry's exploitation of women and constant sexual arousal (a world Sergio found vulgar and undependable), so that she, too, left him alone as his parents and earlier sexual partners ultimately had done.

The wealthy social set of women seeking marriage with men like Sergio tended to view him as more worldly than he was at heart. While ostensibly at ease in every social situation, he took little pleasure in any part of it. As his feeling function developed through analysis, he became so critical of women he knew that I began to sense that his homosexual liaisons had been a retreat from dealing with feminism in its crasser variety, which permeated his social circle to an increasing extent. Yet he began to want to settle into a marriage, and he dreamed of having children whom he could raise in a closely physical and affectionate way, the opposite of his own experience as a child. The danger of his compensation needs in this fantasy was very apparent in analysis, and it will take Sergio much time to settle into a steadier middle-life pattern which will be slow to emerge.

Where some sexual indecision is present, it is clear that the aggressive, explicit, sexual experimentation of feminist upper-class women, turned Sergio away; he didn't see these women as potentially good enough mothers. He also thought of them as "taking," not "giving" partners. His sensitivity, in general, which was outstandingly "human," often could not be spiritually matched by these ambitious, ruling, not very feminine women. Building Sergio's self-confidence was extremely difficult. I had the impression that Sergio's masculinity was intact, but that his homosexual experience fulfilled a variety of his needs that seemed to hold him within a bisexual tendency at this time. His growth has shown in an orientation towards worthwhile social and charitable work; a deeper insight into himself, his shadow and the shadow of his family; and, a determination to be a "good" person, whatever that may be in our time. His religious feeling and his desire to be a father still may lead him into a later and worthwhile marriage. He feels that this might bring deeper love and satisfaction than he has known. The wider boundaries of bisexuality challenge this thus far, and the transient sense of his past relationships disappoint his hopes for the future.

In Sergio's infancy, neither female nor male touching of his body had been so special as to condition a preference for same or opposite gender "skin feeling." Emotions shifted between a nurse reading a bedtime story, caressing his face and kissing him "good night," to a male cook taking Sergio onto his shoulders and showing him what was in the highest kitchen cupboards. It is possible to theoretically ascribe a lack of differentiation in *attraction or taboo* towards gender touch in a child raised without parental demonstration of physical affection, and to suggest that this can bring a dual development of need for the intimate touch of both genders.

As is more rare, where penis erection is emotionally quite easily possible in a male's teenage with either gender, the bisexual pattern, thought to be universal by Freud, becomes quite fixed. It is pluralistic here, in that no greater sense of oneness or unity got established in sexual relations definitively at any stage of Sergio's experience. No partner seemed "enough," "right," or "final" in this developmental sequence.

Bill's Case

The developmental sequence of archetypal movement begins in childhood with the clarification of sex-correlation to the self. The mother, or her surrogate, always represents the self initially. Although my patient, whom I shall rename Bill, was moved across two oceans by the age of three, his mother traveled with him. The mother was emotionally disturbed at the time by her divorce from Bill's father. There was enough of mother's presence, although erratic and undependable, to suggest that at least a partial evocation of the mother archetype had been achieved in projection and introjection by my patient. As effectively there was no father for Bill after about the age of eighteen months, he only remembered a succession of truant lovers in his mother's bedroom. This caused confusion in Bill about detaching from mother; that is, he fantasized that he should protect his mother from her lovers, but as a small boy had no means to do so, and so could not detach himself from a primary sexual sense of relationship to his mother. An older brother who was sent away to boarding school early on had become his only attachment figure, but the brother's nature was unlike a fathering brother, a fraternal one, or an incestuous one. In searching through this early psychohistory, it was loneliness and the lack of meaningful male relationships which suggests the evocation of the father archetype was not called up into a clear image. The search for the father-imago was later acted out in hetero- and homosexual oscillation between an objective, or homosexual, object-seeking and a subjective (both hetero- and homosexual) father-as-self acted out.

Bill's overt sexual pattern started with an early marriage, at twenty-two, to a young businesswoman who traveled away for work for as long as five months at a time. Bill liked the girl initially and experienced good mutual orgasm with her. He left his wife after four years during a period when she was away for her work, having been lured into gay sex by a homosexual. In this relationship Bill also experienced good mutual orgasm. Physically, the sexual orgasmic stakes were equalized between both gender-bodies and persons.

Bill began to advance his professional career and achieved financial independence through work. He seemed relieved to abandon the husband's role. He remembered anal and oral patterns in homosexuality as both outgoing in phallic pleasure and ingoing in receptive pleasure. Neumann remarks, "the mother's breast to the child can be experienced as fatherly and begetting, although her embrace manifests the motherly containing." We can assume how great the damage was in Bill's entire early caring situation but, as his mother was at least present, I would argue that the mother archetype, both "good" and "bad," had been subliminally constellated but not as yet clearly separated from the Great Mother archetype, which was still being experienced as if it were the real mother's image in psyche.

Bill drifted away from his gay partner and next lived with a wealthy woman. He became described as a *gigolo*. He was now forty and promiscuous and there was an atmosphere of the "penis-baby" syndrome around his affairs. He related to his penis almost independently from the rest of his body and wanted a baby by his wealthy lady friend, but she did not conceive. She didn't agree to marry him or anyone else at the time. Soon in an oscillation partly determined by unhappiness and despair, Bill entered a gay relationship with a professional colleague. This latter affair Bill remembered as his first experience of friendship at a deep level, and the sexuality involved seemed somewhat less important than heretofore. His gay friend took a fatherly, caring role, and Bill almost constellated a father-image in the projection within same-sex boundaries onto him. He began to drink quite heavily and swung over to a black African married woman with whom he claimed he found an "even deeper understanding." Bill was now forty-seven. As he wanted children by this woman, the father archetype within him seemed to be developing symbolically with a literal potential. He found in this heterosexual relationship a tenderness he had never known to such an extent. Unfortunately the woman was married, with children of her own, and refused to divorce for Bill. It is noteworthy that Bill chose a married woman who remained unavailable for marriage.

The father archetype may now have begun to influence Bill's inner images of masculinity in a positive way, but its late and partial constellation did not permanently influence his behavior. The male-female uroboros with the male figures initially subordinate to the Great Mother is followed by the struggle of the symbolic male figures to emerge as independent inner masculine images. At this point, Bill met a mirrorimage of himself: a bisexual man with whom he developed an affectionate gay relationship rather than a passionate one. This relationship ostensibly brought Bill into therapy. The new companion "fathered" Bill through financial wealth, and Bill, acquiescing, gave up women altogether in return. This conflict was partly resolved by projecting a father image onto the figure of Mohammed, as Bill joined a Sufi study group and seriously studied Sufism. The patriarchal uroboros, in rising from the client's unconscious, possessed and overwhelmed Eros with a creative form of Logos. For the patient, Sufism became his "creative realm of Logos." Psychologically introjected, this seemed to hold him from his terrible Great Mother complex, his wounded child, and his almost nonexistent real father memories. As European Sufis are not fully acceptable to the Muslim community, the client was still defending himself from male father figures consciously, while unconsciously reaching a bisexual individuation of impressive stature. When Bill's lover became seriously ill, Bill became both man and woman in taking care of him, handling business affairs and feeling quite whole. The work in therapy to repair the wounded child within was now, through synchronous fate, being partly projected onto the sick partner by my patient. This work of sorting out the client's projections and introjections continued after Bill's lover died of AIDS.

To the extent that Bill has reached the patriarchal world

archetypally, this world stresses the upper, nonsensuous body, the spiritual undertaking, the search for meanings. The situation around my client and his Sufism emphasized his development, and I believe the therapeutic work has helped to truly constellate the father archetype at last. Bill is now fifty. An ontogenic process may be long delayed. Originally Bill experienced his real mother in infancy as if she were the world parent or a bisexual. By living out this confusion fully, he delayed conscious realization of the need to split his real mother, as the Great Mother, into a good and a terrible mother. When that split became conscious in Bill during therapy, the transition began to experiencing the father archetype—which I believe to be a primary problem in bisexuality. Before this occurred the patient had the following dream:

Bill's landlord, a married man, a father and friend, had died in the dream. In life, he represented the patient's image-ideal of a balanced fatherly type as well as his dead lover. Here I picked up the theme of "dying in order to live," and felt some hope that we were coming onto the *temenos* where the father archetype could be born and where religious development might be presaged. The second image of the dream confirmed my intimations. Bill's mother appeared with a treasure chest "in which the values of the elders were contained." However, Bill took this chest and somehow lost it. This was the beginning of a breakup of the hold of the matriarchal mother, *as world parents*, on the patient. He could let go and lose the matriarch's symbols of values that had possessed him. The third image of the dream was of Bill prostrating himself before Mohammed. Here the constellation of a religious archetypal father image is presaged by fear, oblation, and respect for the powerful incarnation of a spiritual father, more "solar" than "phallic." The father is reverenced absolutely. I was again made aware of the difficulty that the biological father had never been a clearly remembered image for Bill; so a fatherly and powerful Prophet, the Seal of the Prophets, became a ritual father for whom feelings of sonship could begin to grow and be projected in archetypal images.

Conclusions About Male Bisexuality

The Freudian understanding of bisexuality tends to be a rather fanatical concept construing that sexual play, as it moves to the mouth, anus, or genitals, is regressive if it is not exclusively genital. In bisexuality, the boundaries between body orifices as erotogenic zones are "progressive," but not delimited by one another. Therefore regression, as a concept, loses much of its theoretical or practical relevance. The bisexual describes the experience of body orifices as all flowing nearer to the love object. Body zones, as accented fields, are *polyvalent*, containing psychic, spiritual, individual, automorphous, and social factors. This does not imply regression of zones into a set hierarchy of either "maturity" or "regression."

The Old Testament idea that procreation is the only acceptable reason for sex no longer carries credence in the world. People often seek psychologically meaningful sexual experience which occurs outside the boundaries of reproductive instinct. Cultural delimitation of what that instinct and those behaviors should be is breaking up and gradually being reconsidered (Walsh 1978). One limited sexual concept that one hears about is that overidentification with anima can explain male bisexuality. Animus-anima are not all that sexualize, because the feeling function itself brings a strong sexual component to bear on personality (Hillman and von Franz 1971). Another much too strongly held conception is that heterosexuality will triumph in the end if the analysis of a bisexual is a success. Bill, my patient, always moved repeatedly and resolutely in the opposite direction, from heterosexuality to homosexuality, throughout his history, and was grateful for an analysis that could accept this without manipulation. Where positive animation of both sexual poles is experienced, oscillation and movement to a central bisexual position may occur. I hope that Jungians would contain their sexual prejudices and discuss sexual themes more explicitly as I am doing in this book, in order to further develop theory and to activate ideas gleaned from clinical practice. Neumann has given us one groundwork and a way of extending archetypal theory. He didn't live long enough himself to complete his discussion of psychosexual development.

Androgynous theory may not help us much in bisexual theory in future, because the concretization of the male-female bipolarity in sexual projection is in no way "inferior," as Singer asserts, to the androgynous position of playing-between the energies and qualities described as masculine and feminine (Singer 1976). Singer is tied to quite rigid gender identification as an *a priori* sexually and she seems, by implication only, to deny the bisexual a dignified place in society, because sexuality puts gender theory psychologically into question sexually. Bisexual expression cannot be dismissed as "inferior." This explains nothing more scientifically than that one is denying Eros and is also reifying sexual sublimation. For psychology, the task ahead is to make an ambisexuality comprehensible, and in therapy the true bisexual gives the analyst a possibility for further insight. Bisexuality, within an instinctual archetypal structure, needs restatement, which can include a transcendent sexual influence to gender itself as a living center-dynamic, neither inferior or superior to other sexual modes.

> [S]exuality . . . undergoes a radical psychization which makes it possible for the originally purely instinctive energy to be diverted from its biological application . . . and to deflect it . . . from its immediate goal. (Jung 1937, par. 239)

VI

Midlife Crisis

I ain't what I ought to be, I ain't what I'm going to be, but I ain't what I was.

Plaque on the Wall of a Cowboy Bar

I REMEMBER A PSYCHIATRIST from a London hospital who, when I mentioned the idea of crisis in middle life, asserted there was no such thing. He claimed statistics showed mental strain and breakdown at all ages of the human journey. Thus, he thought C. G. Jung had no basis for his many references to the specialized dangers of the psychological changes he saw in his patients in midlife.

I want to point towards a quality of psychological difficulty and development unique to midlife; I have no interest in the measurement of its quantity, even if that were possible, but am content to observe these phenomena in a great number of middle-aged men. If overtones and undertones of the midlife crisis exist throughout life's other stages, before and after, the intensity of a change of consciousness during the transition from the first half of life to the second enables its aspects to be more clearly analyzed at that time.

Infancy, childhood, adolescence, and young adulthood prepare the critical period of a midlife *rite de passage;*

mature adulthood, later age and old age continue its solution. If the ego goes beyond the death of the body, as I suspect it does, a resolution within the self may bring a transcendent integration of a person's individuation that the
psyche, during life, attempts to reconsider, redirect, and reaf-
firm through the vicissitudes of the midlife crisis. Even
when a child may have been well analyzed, the midlife crisis
may occur. The very personal begins to become the transpersonal at this time.

Traditionally, Jungians have referred to mythology and
anthropology to amplify and illustrate their psychological
method. An important but small proportion of Jungian analysts still recognize religion as a "given" in the psyche and
carefully include its presence in their work. But if amplification becomes excessive, it may blur Jungian interpretation
both to patients and to the public. Wide amplification is
valid to the ecology of Jungian thought generally; however, I
want to speak quite directly to the call for help those in
midlife crisis experience.

Direct experience teaches us, if we analyze and synthe-
size it sufficiently, how to be empathic to others as we intro-
spect from our own memory that which our own version of
entry upon middle-life experience has entailed. The "feel" of
the situation is what Jung knew about, and that is what concerned him. He always believed his patients' descriptions
were the psychological landmarks from which he could map
out empirical formulations. Where contemporary analysts
underestimate both patients' interpretations and their colleagues' report of cases as empirical "fantasy," they do
everyone damage because they have stopped listening both
to others and to themselves. Where one is deeply and widely
experienced in life in the world—and only such a person
should be a Jungian analyst—he or she is less likely to let
unbridled fantasy enter their own thinking, feeling, intuition, or sensation. As a phenomenologist I can only speak of
what I observe during crisis in middle age, whether in myself, in others, in the analysis of myself by others, or in my
patients in Jungian analysis. Jung's great concern for the
midlife crisis merits constant awareness. It is a critical psychological state. The ramifications of this reach back to the

womb and forwards towards the veil of death. They will only be touched upon here.

For men the time of establishing themselves in the world is started and often established by the age of thirty-five to forty, but, a new crisis of identity can then emerge. Men begin to ask themselves more about the meaning of their lives, of what they actually feel for others close to themselves and for society at large. If they have fought in the military, they may have a very new view of power politics and the fate of Everyman within these forces, and may have to reexamine their own way of life when returning home and into working life. The transitional years between thirty-five to fifty are often a time of spiritual advancement or a crisis of belief that give major psychological problems and changes a new intensity.

More men come to me for analysis in their late thirties than at any other age. They feel that more of themselves can emerge, and that the belief in a total and free honesty in speaking of spiritual matters, health, money, and self, while working analytically with a man, can help them understand what path may be possible to take. Often, until men reach their late thirties, their one-sided ego drive and willful determination have cut them off from self-realization. They surprise themselves with new behaviors of which they didn't believe themselves capable. When trouble ensues, they turn to a therapist who can keep confidentiality and who may interpret their dreams to bring a new contact with their unconscious dimension. Neither the priest nor the psychiatrist can interpret dreams with the aims, authority, and authenticity of the Jungian analyst, who uses techniques of amplification unknown to any other discipline.

Even when a man has a firm religious belief, or a spiritual calling and reasonably civilized behavior (which has become quite rare these days), he often feels a new drive to ask why man can be so violent. Analysis deals with the opposing forces of unresolved mental conflict; but, until these can be glimpsed, men tend to blame others for problems which may grow unconsciously out of themselves. Example helps men more than advice. Friendship based within mutual interests helps men to see themselves as others see them and to

correct some of their false pretension, inflation, and mis-
placed enthusiasms.

The competitiveness of establishing status and achievement, continuing throughout a man's life, seems more
acute, more needed, and a very emotional aspect in the lives
of men under forty. Aging means abandoning the wild ex-
cesses of the body, where sex, drink, light drugs, or a pro-
longed exhaustive sport can no longer be experienced without awareness of the body's limits. The honeymoon with our
health, easy and taken for granted, is over. Sadness, depression, or disillusion may accompany the realization that
moderation must come in the body's use from then on into
older age. At the mid-forties, these questions begin to push
men towards an inner journey, seeking a quality of life they
may have missed on the outer journey. This atmosphere and
quality of life become more important, and personal and professional sacrifices become greater in its name. The question
of loyalty to one's past pushes men to both greater mistakes
and frustrations, as well as to greater growth within. The ultimate philosophical questions about the meaning of life are
recycled; what in earlier days were heated debates of firmly
held opinions with others' differing ideas now begin to require a deeper resonance of selfhood in their consideration.

When it is achieved, this shift of consciousness can prepare men for a second half of life that gains further dynamic
energy and expression from a freer self-knowledge and a freedom from earlier complexes. In a way it is man's last opportunity for a drastic psychological change, as the gradual wan-
ing of mental and physical powers begins to be felt by men
after the age of fifty. Often, the focus of concentration and
the sustaining of working energy is steadier than in one's
forties, but the gradual path towards the sunset of life has its
portents in growing needs to be understood by those closest
to one. Linear time pushes the spirit of average men to grow
up finally, and it is near the age of sixty that men truly become the great teachers and leaders of mankind. (I obviously
exclude here the earlier development of the great religious
prophets and of certain political, artistic, or scientific ge-
niuses.) What they then feel and say has the experiential
power of authenticity, a quality of greater influence than is
sometimes realized. The older man stops flirting with fate

and lives more fully, but carefully, in whatever way he feels possible as fulfillment.

What hinders a smooth passage from the first half of life to the second? At midlife, a shift of consciousness occurs that is both inner and outer. Whatever the outer appearance of circumstance in a man's life, a shift of inner values comes where what seemed evident or taken for granted no longer holds firmly. This is the time for reassessment, realignment, and an initiatory experience that begins the new ground of the second half of life. Initiation is always self-made in the ultimate personal self. It may be assisted in societies by groups, priests, shamans, analysts, lovers, elders, or witch-magicians, but each man must reach the new inner realization within himself: having reached the second half of life one must carry the responsibilities for further self-realization.

To be stuck in the values of the first half of life leads to that unfortunate but oft-seen creature, the boy-man. Youthful men are always positive to society, but men who remain boys destroy the serious fabric of a society and continually endanger it. In no country more than in Britain is this danger so apparent. With the loss of so many men in the Second World War, fathering by actual fathers was decimated for a generation. The next generation lost its energy, direction, and much of its common sense through a collective depression. We witness now in British public life many men who have the presence of adolescents or even the "flatness" of prepuberty. These men, although aging and moving into the second half of life, cannot cross the psychological border that manhood requires. One-sided ambition, egocentricity, and rationally limited existence close off these men from the richness of their unconscious possibilities. Clinging to status rather than furthering their relationship to society, these boy-men run the risk of being out of touch with society at large, and are the worst possible leaders for Britain's growth and maintenance. They gradually lose the respect and interest of the public, if they are in public life, not so much because of their ideas but because of their paper-thin personalities and childish appearance.

To cross the border of midlife, one must firstly drop defense. This is supremely difficult but vital to self-

development. One must move away from the limited identity with a one-sided self-image and with one role. The unconscious enters this arena with new intuition for symbolic
and synchronistic events which can lead one forward to dare
to cross new boundaries. This may lead to a dark passage, a
depression, as one realizes that one's life may not be going as
one expected in youth. Anxiety begins over life's limits and
one's own short life. Lassitude, disillusion, and disappointment accompany a sense of loss: one's parents die or one
dies psychologically to one's parents as well. Children reach
puberty and beyond, and will go away. More than this, the
limits of one's own ability are sensed and the omnipotence
of youth must be abandoned. More than humility is required
for dropping false pride and facing later life. One needs to
reach deeply into one's undiscovered intuition to see a way
forward to reach one's fuller potential within, not only the
outward appearance of one's various roles.

Men usually believe that unselfishness is the key to understanding. I would rather say that to reach selfhood, without which one's relationships remain limited and without a
possibility to grow further, a certain careful self-awareness
and reconsideration of what the self actually can do and be
for others is necessary. Selfhood is rarely in midlife what one
earlier thought it would be. Digression, discretion, and a
new calm must inform others of what one's influence now
can be. One learns much by making a last will and testament at this time. In doing this one learns where one places
material help to one's heirs. Also, one comes to realize that
the personal bequests of possessions, carrying spiritual and
personal messages beyond the grave, are not only the mone-
tary gifts that can be transformed at an heir's will or whim.
Surprisingly, tasks such as this inform one of aspects of personality that may not have been realized before. As one thus
symbolically sheds earlier concepts of "what matters," one
loses that self-consciousness in the limited sense of one's
persona, or the mask of one's earlier personal style and
"front" in dealing with others. By letting go of the attachment to earlier ego-identity, one begins to feel freer within.

When one knows what defeat is—and most men have
many defeats within their path of life, (and one's friends die,
earlier or later, to shut doors one had hoped would be

open)—one falls into a new challenge. One cannot go back to that youthful, one-sided, ambitious ego one knew earlier. The way forward is unknown, insecure, perhaps dark. There is, however, a growing sense of selfhood. When this comes one cannot fall back on the old illusions, the old half-baked personality, the old excuses that become maladaptive. Change is in the air, and change is extremely hard for every man.

According to Verena Kast, the Swiss analyst, two tasks arise at midlife. One is learning that the repetition of events will be witnessed in the next generations and that repetition structures the time in relationship to our death of which we are now more aware. The other is that we no longer contribute to the continuation of blaming our parents for everything; we take responsibility and can renounce heroic effort if we wish—we can temper the rate at which we are pushing the stone, like Sisyphus—whom Odysseus described during his trip through the underworld:

> Then Sisyphus in torment I beheld being roustabout to a tremendous boulder. Leaning with both arms braced and legs driving, he heaved it toward a height, and almost over, but then a Power spun him round and sent the cruel boulder bounding again to the plain. Whereon the man bent down again to toil, dripping sweat, and the dust rose overhead.

The supposed goal cannot be reached; the repetition without end is a punishment of the gods. Although repetition brings an order on which one can depend, the hopelessness of achieving the difficult task brings suffering at midlife.

Goethe's text from *Maxims and Reflections* helps us see as positive the compromise of settling our intentions for something different in the second half of life:

> Yet the most wondrous error is one that concerns ourselves and our abilities. It is that we dedicate ourselves to a worthy task, a noble undertaking, that is beyond our abilities. We strive for a goal that we can never attain. [The] Sisyphus-like suffering that one feels as a result of this effort is all the more bitter, the more earnest one's intentions have been. And yet often just when we view

ourselves as severed from our original intentions forever,
we find something else desirable along the way, something
appropriate to us, with which it was actually our lot to be
contented." (Goethe 1963, 12: 516)

In the second half of life, the word "appropriateness" comes
forward in one's decisions. The outspoken, self-indulgent,
egocentric, ruthless way of youth begins to mellow, like an
aged red wine, to a new and deeper taste. Men begin to think
on their own death and therefore more deeply on what life
is. Death belongs to life; it is not separate or different from
it. The fantasies of continuous expansion in one's own success or constant growth of one's influence begin to wane.
One drifts into a new landscape—the terrain of middle age
wherein separation from earlier needs must be lived
through, suffered and let go forever. "We know what we are
but not what we may become," said Hamlet; midlife teaches
us this and we face the future less sure of what it may bring.
This deeper vulnerability is the true birth of humility,
which tends in the first half of life to have been only false
humility, an unfortunate social grace, to be discarded. With
this real and older humility, a new ground of "beingness"
emerges. One's friends notice that one is emerging. A new
undiscovered self begins a subliminal and then more apparent influence.

Maturity can come at fifty. Where would one find it in
most men earlier on? Bravery, yes. Courage, yes. Strength,
yes. Determination, yes. But maturity? That is why parents
always partially fail. Parents cannot be mature, in this sense,
when most have their children in their twenties, thirties,
and forties. No generation has a "chance" unless it reaches
back to its grandparents, its "wise old folk" who can advise,
warn, and suggest the way to hold and transform the trou-
bles and tragedies of life.

Between thirty-five and fifty, repressed contents of the
unconscious arise from the unconscious; once defenses go
down, what one kept hidden from one's self-knowledge appears. These repressions often contain aspects of pathology
that need effort to absorb into a more conscious awareness
of one's mental aberrations. Murray Stein, the Chicago analyst, has written:

The midlife crisis typically brings about the astonishing recognition of our own hidden-away madness. What comes over us unexpectedly, and "inappropriately," in our middle years is a psychological state of affairs that can steal our pride and self-assurance and throw us into doubts about our emotional balance and mental health. Midlife crisis turns persons inside out and tears up their crafted worlds. Mothers and housewives discover Pan in their gardens and workshops, or Dionysus in night classes; figures who come at them with all the force of preposterous and prepossessing gods demanding submission. Professors spy irresistible nixies in their graduate seminars and thrill to new-found libido, to enchanting visions of soulful delight and communion, and before they know it they have abandoned the library and the laboratory to rediscover the road of passion and adventure. Bankers, ministers, stock market operators, matrons, mothers—who will be next to drop the flow and begin responding to the improbable dance of life? (Stein, M. 1983, 1–2)

This suggests adulthood is as developmental as childhood. At midlife the psyche explodes; and in the night in dreams Hermes comes to steal Apollo's cattle. Metaphorically Apollo's cattle are one's achievements, possessions, children, power, position, accomplishments. In the myth Hermes re-enters his mother's cave and lies innocently by his mother, like a cunning newborn who has brought psychological upheaval by changing attitudes to bonds to parents and society, friends and colleagues. The psyche awakens to newly found meanings and choices; freedom is redefined.

Hermes brings trouble, but inventive and creative trouble; he eventually fashions a lyre for Apollo's musicality. Apollo thought he was the older legitimate brother and Hermes the illegitimate upstart, but the upstart presents Apollo with the soulful, perfect instrument—the lyre. Hermes attracts companions to one's midlife crisis that are surprising but valuable. He is the guide who brings one to psychological liminality—that consciousness that is essential to transition. Hermes guides one over boundaries—an existence in flux—which discovers that doorways and thresholds hold a liminal space as one moves through them. This includes the subliminal space that pushes through to consciousness.

The fixed edges of ego get blurred in midlife. There is a sense as we go which relativizes to self that ego is again the babe innocently sleeping in the maternal cave. But it erupts like a volcano, leaving imprints that are new. The ego's heroic defenses become questioned—what is the still undiscovered landscape outside the castle? The archetypal self-organization breaks down, the ego hangs in suspension, like the drawbridge to the self's moated castle. In alchemy this is the death and dissolution of the Old King and the transition to the new Hermetic king, who guides the groping ego to a deeper liminality; mortality is accepted, limits and compromises in the name of self become acceptable, and a new stage of individuation is approached. The ego grieves the loss of the time of the first half of life. The ghosts of the past must be laid to rest. Two forces meet and converge more fully than before—the ego's more thoughtful intentionality and the archetypal images of intention—these meet in synchronicities of fortune or of catastrophe. Walter Otto writes:

> From him [Hermes] comes gain, cleverly calculated or wholly unexpected, but mostly the latter. That is his true characterization. If a man finds valuables on the road, if a man has a sudden stroke of luck, he thanks Hermes. . . . [T]he favorable moments and their profitable exploitation are so much in the foreground that even thieves could regard themselves as his special protegés. (1979, 108)

The Greeks named the synchronistic moment "Hermes." But he comes as an uncanny shadow presence, a figure of the night. When Hermes arrives, the ego is separated momentarily from its fixed attitudes to whom ego has related and where ego seems to have come from or where it is going. Identification with former ego positions is loosened and this causes disturbance in the archetypal layer of psyche: intuitions, fantasies, big dreams, and synchronistic and symbolic events occur to relight the actor on center stage, to bring new self-messages through to liminal ego awareness—an area of unclear edges and new images of psyche's territory.

Immersion in the unconscious creates regressive dangers of remaining caught in a long and involuntary submission to states of the anima, such as symbiotic union with depression, sexually wild cravings and urges, and somatizations of psychological conflict. Midlife liminality gives ego a chance to suspend its anima possession or fight back. The anima reaches the status of a goddess at midlife. One must see this anima clearly. Jung has written:

> [E]very interpretation that comes anywhere near the hidden sense [of the symptom, the impulse, the fantasy, etc.] has always, right from the beginning, laid claim not only to absolute truth and validity but to instant reverence and religious devotion. (1940, par. 266)

To honor the anima, an almost religious struggle is essential for healing as men face the second half of life. To survive this a new birth is needed, one that transforms the earlier needs of the young man. The Self no longer has the inflated and grandiose ideas of men who feel they have unlimited potential. At midlife a core Self assesses more realistically what personal wisdom is, what foundation to life a man now wants. I quote Murray Stein:

> The archetype we are dealing with in considering the experience of a deep-going psychological transformation at midlife is the same as operates in all other transitional periods of life. It is reflected in images of the edge, of boundary lines and borderlines, thresholds, in between spaces and times. And persons whose consciousness is caught up in the force field of this archetype of transition, whenever it occurs, experience liminality with its characteristic and often predictable fantasies, feelings, visions, dreams and even synchronistic events. Mythic imagination saw a master of this mode of existence, of liminality, in Hermes and called him guide of souls and god of thresholds and of passages between realms of existence. So when we say Hermes is present in a situation what we are saying, to put it more pedantically, is that the archetype that was imaged in the mythic figure Hermes is active in this situation as well and is creating these effects. (Stein 1983 , 111)

The persona at midlife moves from the personal, ambitious achiever's mask to a more general and outgoing open face.

Jung describes what happened to him at midlife in a passage written forty-five years afterward:

> When I look back upon it all today and consider what happened to me during the period of my work on the fantasies, it seems as though a message had come to me with overwhelming force. There were things in the images which concerned not only myself but many others also. It was then that I ceased to belong to myself alone, ceased to have the right to do so. From then on, my life belonged to the generality. The knowledge I was concerned with, or was seeking, still could not be found in the science of those days. I myself had to undergo the original experience in the soil of reality; otherwise they would have remained subjective assumptions without validity. It was then that I dedicated myself to the service of the psyche. I loved it and hated it, but it was my greatest wealth. My delivering myself over to it, as it were, was the only way by which I could endure my existence and live it as fully as possible. (Jung 1961, 192)

In depth, it behooves one to speak of the agonies of the soul; for the search for life's available meanings is never more intense in men's lives than when fifty approaches. The pivotal and profound question emerges yet again, "Who am I?"

This agonizing query can set in motion a time of dying to the first half of life in order to live the second half in ripeness and readiness, for "the readiness is all." We cannot know what happiness and what travail may come, but we can be ready with humility and renewed strength for the harvest of the season of midlife. The colors of life's autumn begin to emerge into one's psychology; one finally learns something of patience, of acceptance, of quiet and unknown sacrifice, and a new self-valuing not in selfishness but in further self-availability to others, not only in acts, but in one's very presence and way of being. One faces the darkness, one's weakness, one's ongoing limits, one's lacks, one's addictions to self-created barriers within and without. One sees oneself more fully and accepts what one is. This must be the first step within the second half of life. Forgiveness of self becomes important—one was what one was; but, now, one can be what one is. Hallelujah! Freedom! Self-knowledge! *The light is darker, but the dark is lighter.*

This initiation may come through indications in dreams, visions, physical and mental illness, change of place and kind of life both personally and in work, and in a new religious conversion or spiritual commitment to others and to one's self. Once this road is taken, the psyche cannot again turn back to less than a greater realization of one's own personality.

> But they that wait upon the Lord shall renew their strength; they shall mount up with wings as eagles; they shall run, and not be weary; and they shall walk, and not faint. (Isaiah 40:31)

VII

Loneliness and the Approach of Death

Men must endure
Their going hence, even as their coming hither.
Ripeness is all.

Shakespeare, *King Lear*

AS MUCH AS AGGRESSION offers itself as a choice, I believe loneliness to be the problem of our time. There have never been substitutes for human contact, an absorbing kind of work, and an awareness of God. The ability and willingness to communicate is a prime prerequisite to avoiding loneliness. Men often repress this loneliness by constant occupation (as a preoccupation) at a cost

> of a narrowing and warping of the personality, because the person concerned becomes identified with his function, his social status. He ceases to be a human being and becomes a politician, pimp, priest, pundit, pariah, sales executive, civil servant, industrialist, housewife, wolf, what-not. So it is seen that much of our human behavior derives from the avoidance of loneliness. (Hoskisson 1963, 28)

There are several kinds of loneliness that may be specific in their typology. The desire for compatible companionship leads men into extramarital affairs when their wife no longer gives enough sexual compatibility, and may lead in a minority of men to buying the time and bodies of prostitutes. Men seek in prostitutes the sexual experiences outside the range their wives will consider, often seeking more oral-genital stimulation, more variety of vaginal or anal intercourse postures, and a greater physicality less connected to spirituality, sensitivity, and responsibility.

Often unhappy husbands are lonely because they lack a satisfactory hope, cause, goal, or faith. The psyche needs a teleological goal for its ongoing sense of renewal. Through disillusion or a lack of determined staying power, a man may take up but then discard politics. "[They] leave the party, they join the *avant garde* of some art form for a time, later to take up eugenics, eurhythmics, nudism, food reform, peace pledge, marriage guidance" (Hoskisson 1963, 31). These men often give their names to charity organizations and, for a time, work for a cause. Then a faithless kind of loneliness sets in. Not apathetic or totally disinterested, these men shift into discounting and discrediting their own efforts in time, and so become quietly destructive. Their integrity is in doubt. They cannot both be identified with and yet partly free from their "good works."

Often these men develop fantasies about their loneliness and also fantasies of others' loneliness through novels, theatre, television, and films. They make of real people a fantasy of what they desire and require, projecting onto unsuitable partners a wished for, but unrealistic ideal illusion. When relationships fail for reasons of fantasy projection, men tend to feel completely cut off, and lose a hope which they have only ever partially experienced.

Loneliness is not solitude. Loneliness is more the conscious sense of separation from an achievement or a realized relationship with someone needed, required, desired. Much of this inability to break through to contact, to make the effort towards satisfying relatedness, requires attention. Where attention fixes on self-pity, nothing moves in psyche. Loneliness is dispelled in the real consideration and compassion for another person, so we can see loneliness as a breakdown in communication. Communication requires attention to give and receive, to be willing to be a cause and an effect in life. Neuroticism always involves a lack of attention to one-self or to others. It tends to obsessive regard and disregard of self or other, often on a fluctuating basis. The psychotic goes further: attention is paid to a self-created frame of reference mostly unrecognizable to others, using one's own concepts and one's own distorted language (a "word-salad"). If feelings, emotions, and ideas fall outside a frame of reference, a man loses affinity, mutual attraction, and kindly reciprocal feelings. He will be rejected on grounds that he is diabolical and tedious, beyond others' understanding. Then a man will feel that constant rebuff means one is not wanted by anyone, and he will contract out of social intercourse. Uncertainty leads to a loss of effectiveness.

> We are unconsciously aware of this need for certainty and the whole of our lives we are struggling for it. I could cite you hundreds of psychological experiments that prove this point. One simple one is by Mischotte in which he projected a frame of light onto a screen and then threw a spot of light into the center of it. He then moved the frame of light about, so that the relationship of the frame to the spot varied. The spectators were convinced that it was the spot that moved, because they had accepted the rectangle as their frame of reference. Our whole perceptive mechanism is an attempt to make us feel certain. One of the most terrible experiences you can have is to wake up and really not know where you are. Yes, certainty is closely related to our capacity to make and maintain personal relationships. (Hoskisson 1963, 82)

In being, a man can go on doing: in doing a man may end up having. Or he may not. Fate, fortune, always play into a man's having; it is culturally a truth that society sets its economic systems so very few can end up having—whether in capitalism where tax takes away, socialism where egalitarian bureaucratic power takes away, or communism where buddies of the tyrant take all away. Our male obsession for having, as a pecking-order badge, may lead to the appalling failure of not getting enough to satisfy ambition's insatiability. If men increase their action only to have, we end up in ecological disaster, the rape of resources to serve the few who may have historically killed to control the resource—as long as it lasts.

It is a lonely position to control vast wealth and thereby power. It separates one from normal communication, as all other men beneath in the pecking order will only peck away at you in reality or in negative fantasies. They will envy, conspire against, be jealous of, and ultimately connive a way to usurp the throne of prestigious raw power. Material power, and the belief that the here and now is all, have added a lonely and haunted aspect to life, the result of greed in most successful men today. The machine-like men of achievement and the puppet-like behavior of their preferred slaves leaves me in little doubt that men need to reexamine what "success" actually is in life. If we personally reach out unendingly for an increased production and grasping of wealth that cannot eventually be there because of drained resources everywhere in the world, that greed will lead to a total breakdown of everyone and everything known. Men will continue to be dissatisfied only with money politics. The Orthodox Church survived seventy years of official non-existence in Russia as the purely materialistic manipulation of economy failed to satisfy thousands of men's and women's spiritual longings related to an historically established form of worship—orthodox Christianity.

The monotheisms are not attempts of men to fuse with God, but a realization of the unity-within-variety of all levels of human beings. Religion is an attempt to connect to the truths of creation and to acknowledge this Oneness. Faith brings with it a deep assuaging of loneliness, because the other-as-God encompasses all beings and manifestations are related to oneself. There is then no sense of being cut off, but an entrance to an immanent psychology of both being and belonging, at all times and regardless of apparent circumstance. When this is realized to be as true for one's brothers and sisters as for oneself, the awakening sense of the truly *fraternal* enables a give and take within the relativity of dignity and justness before the witness of Godhead. With God as one's witness it is very difficult to be as lonely as it may be without this monotheistic awareness. Freud's great loneliness was that he thought the only witness of human behavior was the relative force of sexual energy. He deified an instinct as the god.

For Jung, the incomparable and less relative witness of Godhead—within and without—became a certainty which kept Jung (potentially) in touch with all myths, all symbols, and all social and cultural behaviors historically basic to man's expression. This fraternal oneness could give men back a role in which their total psychic energy was seen to have not only an instinctual pole but, complementarily, a spiritual pole as well. This continuum of man's psychic energy from instinct to spirit could then contain the energy that results in all human action without limit and without displacement onto, or dispersal into, what it was not. Jungian psychology existentially erases loneliness by enormously enlarging man's awareness of himself *in potentia*. The task of individuation can always be carried further, therefore "stuckness" is immanently temporary to the goal of life. With self-development can come a connectedness to the many within the one, a lasting companionship to life itself which potentially enhances relationship and keeps loneliness more as a feeling of temporary regression, not an experience which can continue itself as total and lasting.

A part of a companionship with life needs to be a preparation for death. In my neighborhood in London a distinguished modern teaching hospital was built some years ago for a multi-million pound budget. When completed it was discovered that no room for the dead had been included in the plan! These plans had been studied by a panel of consultant physicians, senior nurses, and administrators for years; they were not the work of architects alone. Yet medical practitioners, who constantly are with dying patients, had repressed the idea of a morgue in their new hospital. Architects and contractors had also forgotten about death. What a perfect example of man's ability to live as if death were not always a possible instant away.

The intensity and beauty of human life is experienced partly because life is but a reprieve from death. Everything in physical life sinks into a physical death. We have to shed our bodies; our extremely crude burial customs, of dropping caskets underground or cremation, belie our lack of respect for the dead and their possible "shades" among us. Funeral services become shorter and more cursory by the decade. We seem so accelerated that to stop for a funeral is like giving up an addiction—it takes energy and forbearance to publicly grieve a death.

Yesterday, in the small town in Spain on the Mediterranean coast where I write these words, the funeral of an eleven-year-old boy was held. He had lit a cigarette in a hut he had built of beach straw and, stumbling backwards, had become trapped in a resultant fire that took his young life. The village suddenly totally stopped. The few hundred residents all left their work the next day to line the approach to the Catholic chapel where a high funeral mass was spoken. The mayor came. The street cleaner came. We foreigners came. In the hard provincial life of a poor beach town, the sense of death was both personal for each and for all together. The open car serving as a hearse was covered with white lilies and carnations, a floral tribute fit for a king. Here no one repressed their grief. Men and women openly wept as the bereft family entered the chapel. Relatives staggered and fell to their knees wailing. An ancestral past that includes the fervor of Spanish and Arab blood gives the Andalusian Spaniards a deep awareness of the life and death struggle. A large police force from the province controlled traffic, the crowds, the collective atmosphere of suffering. Here in the rising "second" World there was no illusion, no repression. Human and religious philosophies combined to honor the passing of a young soul; people gathered to honor his family and, as witnesses in solidarity, together to think upon death and its mystery.

As men grow toward their dying, they begin to feel they have lived their share. They begin to hand over to the next generation their portion of wisdom and mature presence. Whether younger men avail themselves of this advice from the old men of a community depends greatly on local social, ethical, and moral values, which vary widely across the world. I have always been interested in those men who voluntarily help aged men on a regular basis. What return they glean on the investment of their time, their kindness, their hearts, in conversation with those ailing older men of "former" generations is great indeed. Considering the vicissitudes of a long life, it cannot be easy for an old man to be sure of what to suggest to the younger man following along. There are so many pitfalls along the way. Dwelling on tragedy may balance the encouragement to persevere that most grandfathers tend to offer their grandsons. Looking backwards through lived experience is a great contrast to looking forward in projection. Young men think the tragedies "won't happen to me." Lack of realized success is also put aside by the young, "I'll show them" being the one-sided call of will, determination, and heroic achievement.

Where older men have their life partners still by their side, a companionship of deeply-moving trust, consideration, and forbearance can be seen in retirement communities, where the old live in remarkable peace and harmony. Where money is in short supply, the tensions of a restricted lifestyle are often overcome by the rich memories carried by the old and the discovery of simple pleasures. Passing the time becomes an art, not just an existence. Many charities offer older people a chance to share in local area work and certain very socially minded employers have the social conscience to offer the aged suitable part-time work. Retirement becomes a reflective period, often busy with appropriate exercise, family visits, community groups, and private social life. Yet the strain of deteriorating physical prowess constantly makes itself felt, and great courage and patience is required to live with a metabolism that is shutting-down.

Alertness and feeling about the news of the day seems to keep the older aged a part of the "now," even if only as witness and spectator to fast-changing conditions. The sense of "having seen it all before" often prevails, as each generation fails to learn from the former and the same crises and tragedies are again relived and borne. Where there are regrets of things not lived out or not tried, it is helpful to the younger to learn of this and to consider whether they are running a similar risk of leaving certain aspirations too late. It enables one to check one's priority list against those who may feel they got it partly wrong.

It is unfortunate that few contemporary societies have a group of elders being really seriously listened to by younger men in power positions. The demands of power today in overpopulated nations mean younger, middle-aged men are taking critical leadership in positions formerly reserved for the more experienced. Computer communication has speeded up the whole area of public relations so that a leader's popularity is being tested in polls almost day by day. Youthful media image is pushed by the publicity-mongers. The acceleration of change is thus pushed yet faster, leading to what begins to feel like a collective hysteria. Money buys television advertising time so it speaks more loudly than ever. Many men turn away from public responsibility because reputation can be bought by television advertising merchants. Images can be altered, enhanced, lied about, faked by skillful television ads and appearances that become more important to public figures than the promised platforms of their public work, stance, and responsibility.

Stance is the word. It is a time when media stance is taken as fact, no matter how it is contrived or manipulated for propaganda purposes. If the printed word used to be believed, now it is the media contortion of the facts that is believed. For wasn't "seeing is believing" always the bottom-line response of a doubting public? Yet camera angles, atmosphere contingency, cutting out half of the interviewee's statements from television, and obscuring that which is not photographed by repressing it from public view are but a few of the trickster-like techniques that prevail in media image-building today. In order to adjust to a new, fast-paced, nightmare reality of publicity campaigns in the name of internationally allied sectors, nations, regions, cities, consortiums, and individuals, we must begin to ask, "Is what we saw on television news reporting to be believed?" Truth has become the "needle in the haystack."

The elderly must try to learn a new jargon, a new pace, a new manner of sifting the TV debacle of truths, half-truths, half-baked truths, and non-truths that flash across the screens of millions of retirement homes—whether private or community-based. This may conflict with early conditioning, with tightly-held moral, religious, and social convictions that cannot be altered in the elderly person's psychic equilibrium and economy in the closing stages of life. Often, ego boundaries tighten defensively in the aged, a natural conservation of restricted availability of psychic energy. In men, a softer masculinity may emerge, or a more crotchety and nervous aggression usually seen in less healthy and less integrated individuals.

These personality aspects revolve around sexual issues as well as spiritual developments. Men seem not to experience so striking a change of life as women report in their menopause or climacteric. In their fifties, most men have a lower level of testosterone than before, but this change is gradual and relatively small compared to female hormonal change at menopause. Changes in male sexual arousal are reported by the Kinsey Institute and may include

> needing more time and more direct stimulation of the penis for getting an erection and reaching orgasm, erections that may be less firm, and testicles that may not elevate as high up in the scrotum during arousal. At ejaculation, there may be less semen and orgasmic muscle spasms may be less intense. It is also common for men to feel less of a need to ejaculate during each sex act and the refractory period (the time between one ejaculation and the next time a man can ejaculate again) may increase. (Reinisch and Beasley 1991)

It is encouraging for the aging to note that men who have had earlier problems with premature ejaculations during intercourse will benefit from a lowered urgency to ejaculate and may be able to extend coition for longer lengths of time. The new stimulation technique needed for penile erections often leads to greater imaginative stimulation of the woman as well, so that both partners find increased possibilities of sexual enjoyment and enhancement.

Spiritually, men may find their quieter older life brings them into a peaceful contact with women, a more mutual contact in which competition between genders brings no social or economic advantage. In this sense, a more "hermaphroditic" atmosphere may prevail in groups of the aged, with a resultant humor and good-heartedness between genders that is more sex-free and less fraught with sexual gesture, attitude, and language, and more concerned with general feeling values, levels of well-being, and platonic relationship. Whichever way a man may go in his late-age behavior, sexual drive and desire continue at a slower pace in most men to the end of their lives. Where a much-loved partner dies, many men return to masturbation, not desiring the replacement of their memory of their wives by another woman; many widows feel the same way about replacement males.

With the loss of a principal partner, men face a loneliness and solitude that is a great challenge. Often a displacement onto grandchildren, if there are such living nearby, becomes rather exaggerated; a man is relieved not yet to face in very young grandchildren the problems he lived through with his own children. He will "dote" on his grandchildren as his last rather passionate response to relationship. Sons and daughters may suffer in this one-sided show of preference from lonely grandfathers for their grandchildren as the last moments of time for better relationships to their own children are quickly ticking away. Death is around the corner, and too much is often left unsaid or unlived between fathers and sons and fathers and daughters. The overgrowing of lasting Oedipal tensions may need adjusting, and old wounds on all sides may need further forgiveness and understanding. Where a father can release his children by a deep acceptance of their difference of temperament, gifts, lifestyles, and moral, social, and religious choice, you have that rare man whose fatherhood has included a deeply internal side of consideration, generosity, and commitment to his own children. As fathers can learn more today from psychology's increased understanding that a loving father must have "the capacity to accept a baby's right to bring him all its needs, wishes, fantasies and feelings but not to expect the baby to deal with his own mainly unconscious needs, wishes, fantasies and feelings that are inappropriate to that relationship" (Layland 1981). One of the qualities the good-enough father will have had is to realize what he may expect and what he has no reason to expect from his children. Where egos are weak in older men, they will want constant shows of affection and extraverted respect from children. Where greater self-maturity has been reached, an older man will release his children from ego demands, and accept their own adulthood by treating them as separate but especially loved individuals. This task continues for a man if he has living children to the final moments of his life. Men in this sense never shed responsibility. It is in-built if they have family, and men carry these relationships to the grave.

In its idealistic concept of the male, society sets a very hard task. It wants both mental gifts and powerful physicality from men, yet it expects loving and faithful relationships to be lived with a wife and children. It wants a man to share and ultimately to give all his earnings to his family. It expects men to be firm in authority, tender in love, faithful in responsibility, steady in constant example, and it wants men to fight unto death if a society is attacked by an enemy from outside its domain. Men come into a world full of demands made upon them, from the earliest admonition to be "a good little man" before they can scarcely walk. I believe that men should radically reconsider whether society's demands upon them are not now too destructive to natural man's psyche for his survival. Men, within their on-flowing sexuality, are experiencing a partial psychological castration in a materialist and rather barbaric civilization. This is a situation that will lead on to an eventual overwhelming compensating aggression from all men expressed towards everyone in sight!

We know many men shift this aggression into a displacement onto extremes of worldly ambition, which their families or friends aid or abet. Money brings living space, armed security, certain "friends" in the legal system, and the chance to rule. Money cannot buy spiritual insight, true love, compassion between generations, perfect health, immortality, or happiness. These more elusive prizes are not aggression's reward. They are in the domain of psychological growth, which collective man/woman continues to resist, partly through despair and partly because society is deeply afraid of psychology, the education of the individual soul from its unconscious sources, and afraid of the change this could bring to an emancipation of men from being pawns in the cogs of their exploitation by others—that wheel upon which most men are torn asunder from their natural worth.

Epilogue

WHEREVER ONE TOUCHES the deepest sexual instincts, which also encompass the spiritual need of men, there is no limit as to where the story begins or ends. Each man has his own unique need for sexual expression, his own fate as to whom the partners of that experience have been or will be, and his own equation of how important his sexual life has been within his total experience and to his experience of totality. One man's dessert is another man's poison.

I am indebted to my male analysands over many years of analytic work for releasing to me any clinical or personal material this book contains. The trust afforded me, and the hard work my patients have given their therapy, has enabled me to choose the areas this book has discussed as the most pressing in interest for the majority of men and women. The future of sexuality will depend on the genetic health of the races, particularly concerning the immune system as we cope with levels of stress and ecological damage new to mankind. It also will always depend on the psyche, its desires, balances, complexes, neuroses, and pathologies. The story of sexuality within psyche unfolds endlessly, as does the cosmos itself.

Sex has an image darkly forming upon which all men gradually shed light as they experience its relation not only to body, but also to soul and spirit.

Appendix

THE FOLLOWING TEXT, from pages 154–61 of my 1988 book, *The Self in Early Childhood,* is reprinted with the kind permission of its original publishers, Free Association Books.

A self/not-self awareness may in the first place be concerned with or about defence. If one accepts Jung's archetypal theory and considers the archetypes as interrelated constituents of the self which would have a teleological aspect of serving the individual as a whole, then the self would have a defensive or protective role towards itself at a more basic level, and definitely so in the infant in advance of full ego-development. A weak ego would be overwhelmed both by powerful archetypal unconscious material and by the impinging outer world of objects.

To recognize not-self the self would need to possess a great number of items of information, referred to in biology as "the message." The message, on present knowledge, is encoded in the structure of genes made up of deoxyribonucleic acid (DNA) in a folded, double spiral shape. The message-carriers are believed to be a type of ribonucleic acid (RNA) and in a chain shape determined by the pattern of DNA. Psychologists and biologists tend to agree that these messengers may be in the form of templates, enzymes, hormones, genes, catalysts, or pheromones.

These diverse messengers are described in theories relevant to them by appropriate or acceptable terminology:

The psychological message concerned: (1) a diversity of specific responses to stimuli from what is not-self; (2) it must be all-pervasive so as to reach all defence outposts; (3) it enables the individual to recognize what is imposed not-self even if the self shares with the not-self certain features; (4) . . . it prohibits the wrecking of elements of the system as if they were extraneous (Stein, L. 1967, 104).

In biology the defence system is a somatic system with four analogous characteristics to the four psychological aspects of messages described above (Burch and Burwell, 1965): (1) the somatic defence system shows a wide range of specificity; (2) its agents are ubiquitous or pervasively present; (3) this system recognizes the not-self; (4) in predisposed persons, the agents can attack self-tissue in a "misguided" way which is presumed to be at the root of autoimmune disease. As neither the nervous nor the endocrine system is able to fulfill all these functions, Burch and Burwell assume that the biological analogue of the self would be the lymphoid stem cells and/or the undifferentiated mesenchyme cells of the reticuloendothelial system (Gell 1957). There are data consistent with such a postulation of some psychosomatic equivalence between stem cells and self without any intention of indicating that there is a lateral psychophysical parallelism between the self-archetypes and endothelial systems which is autonomous and free from total nerve control (as the self is also thought to be in terms of its superordinate function). Neither hormonal nor nervous systems store or carry information that allows a secondary response: for example, antibody production can go on months or even years after the first immunization. Stein (1967) points out that this reminds one of belated psychological reactions to trauma in early childhood. However, even if deposited patterns in the nervous and endocrine systems are not thought to be paralleled by those borne by the self, this would not prevent functions like conscious acts or symbolization from being delegated to the former systems.

Anatomically, the lymphatic system is described by Burch and Burwell (1965) as correctly qualified to serve as a defence against not-self. Random disordering, due to the enormous complexity of the genetic message, could be found in the stem cells. Medawar (1957) points out that evidence supports the theory that the antigenic substance which stimulates antibody formation is DNA, from which chromosomes are made. If inoculated, DNA can bring about genetic transformation and behave as if it were a gene.

This idea of immunological mistakes is important to these general considerations. For example, in mammals the unborn offspring obtains necessary nutriment by sharing the mother's blood circulation in the womb. But if cells from the embryo's blood pass the barrier of placenta and enter the mother's bloodstream, antibody function can be induced. If these reenter the baby's blood, haemolytic disease or damaged red blood corpuscles can result. Another example would be chronic inflammation of the thyroid gland where autoimmune disease sets in, a condition where the organism erroneously or to its detriment destroys a needed constituent as if it were not needed. In thyroid inflammation as described by Burnett (1962) the gland has been invaded by lymphocytes which release antibodies and ultimately render the thyroid useless.

The distinction which enables the organism to recognize self and distinguish it from not-self may depend on the stereochemical fit of the "mirror image" with which the organism is confronted. Steric shape refers to the different positions in space which atoms occupy within molecules of the same chemical constitution. Differences of steric shape are characteristic of amino acids on which life depends (Libby 1965). An identity of stereochemical fit could be schematically assumed when an object characterized by troughs and peaks is turned to its "mirror image," so that its troughs and peaks correspond. Complementarity would reverse the object and mirror image so that peaks face troughs and vice versa.

This idea of two types of fit would account schematically for the maintenance of biological identity when either the self-archetype or the lymphocyte encounters are a not-self pattern of either type fit in mirror image. In the identity-type fit of Fordham's deintegration theory, involving quick reintegration of an object when there is a good fit, would be the archetypal self theory in analogy; psychosomatically, the process whereby the original whole or self becomes structured into interrelated elements (or messengers) occupying certain postulated preferred stations (statistically) would be an identity-type fit.

Fordham describes the second or complementarity type of steric fit, when the correspondence between object and deintegrate of self is not exact. At first the object will not be perceived at all, but a tolerance develops so that the object is later perceived even when it does not fit the deintegrate (Fordham 1957). In view of the examples given in autoimmune disease, with their disastrous consequences, it must be said that in immunity theory the non-fitting object is an antigen or toxin. A toxin is toxic because its structure is in some sense a complementary fit to a genetically predetermined ones.

Burnett (1962) assumes that the function of the antigen is to stimulate a preexistent pattern into activity. In Fordham's theory of deintegration this is precisely what the object does to the self as a preexistent structure at birth. Just as at first a foreign substance may be accepted by the organism, the repeated injection stimulates an antibody into action, and when injected, antibodies provoke an immunological response. It is not surprising that the steric fit necessary for genetic stability can become pathological if changes develop from an identity to a complementary relation. This happens if an immature organism (the infant) is presented with a foreign substance as if it were a part of the self. When the self knows that the object stands in a relation of complementarity to the archetypal image, the host will not tolerate the object.

An example of complementary opposites and their possible incompatibility is Parrish's (1966) work on sperms and ovum in infertile women. In four of forty-eight infertile women, destructive antibodies specific to the plasma coating of their husbands' sperm was produced. Biologically, complementarity can lead to a violent reaction.

An important example of this is reported by Turnbull and Hawk (1966) in the study of regional ileitis in the colon. Unlike chronic ulcerative colitis, in colonic ileitis the mucous membrane is not primarily involved. Rather, the self appears to be destroying the colon as not-self via the lymphatic and reticuloendothelial systems. Acheson and Truelove (1961) found that the disease often attacked patients suffering from a conflict between the need for dependence and the family's ideal of independence. A period of immaturity unduly shortens the time for digested (or interjected) not-self material to be accepted, and psychoimmunological tolerance is not developed. Twice as many of the patients they studied who had destructive diseases of the digestive tract were weaned from the breast during the first month of life as in the control group, who had later weaning.

In viewing the principle of self/non-self recognition, the essential problem is that when tolerance of self-antigens breaks down, autoimmune deficiency syndrome may develop. Inappropriate responses to innocuous antigens such as pollen may give rise to allergic hypersensitivity. In some infections, immune reaction to resistant microorganisms may damage tissue as much as the infection itself does. Advantageous immune reactions may shift to hypersensitivity, as both mechanisms have an underlying similarity.

Whether an antigen is eventually accepted as self or rejected as not-self is partly dependent on timing: antigens are accepted as self if they persist long enough. In the embryo, it may be that any antigen that is present through the immune systems maturation will be accepted as self. If lymphocytes are tolerated at an immature stage they may only later develop a capacity to be immunized. But in the adult, even with mature lymphocytes present, tolerance can be induced with some antigens, such as foreign immunoglobulins, when no adjuvant stimulus is also present. The tolerance/immunity decision is vitally influenced by adjuvanticity of stimuli; most antigens will produce a primary response but these will produce tolerance if injected in many large doses over time. When lesser doses are given over the same time, this often potentiates the immune response instead. The operation of immunological circuits, as to triggers and adjuvanticity of timing, is so complex that as this book goes to press AIDS (acquired immunodeficiency syndrome) is on the increase without a vaccine antidote.

From the layman's point of view the difficulties in comprehending the most basic immunological aspects of the prevention of viral disease, and particularly of AIDS, is formidable. In the first phase of the immune system's response to viral attack there is a non-antigen-specific response of interferons and natural killer cells, but at the same time the virus-infected cells are susceptible to a lysis of the natural killer cells. As the virus replicates, the production of humoral antibodies begins and there is an activation of T-cells that can have a positive or negative effect on the function of immunity. Cytotoxic T-cells may lyse with virus-infected cells or may induce a delayed type of hypersensitivity.

T-cells develop under activation from the thymus when they are induced to become T-lymphocytes. Upon maturation the T-lymphocytes recognize differences between foreign cells and foreign antigens and self-cells and self-antigens. T-lymphocytes are mobile, and after circulating through the blood and lymph pass into body tissues, where they detect foreign substances such as bacteria, fungi, protozoa, and virus-infected cells. They attack foreign substances by producing chemical messengers, the lymphokines, which increase the function of phagocytic defence cells and fight foreign substance in many ways.

B-cells are the other major system of the immune response. They appear first in foetal liver, then in adult bone marrow, and are precursors of plasma cells where production of antibodies and immunoglobulin occurs. T-lymphocytes' products influence the antibodies produced by B-lymphocytes, which interact in a sequence with special proteins, named "complement proteins." The proteins are precursors of enzymes that can initiate inflammation, lyse foreign cells, facilitate phagocytosis, and neutralize or destroy viruses.

These two systems, T and B, influence each other both positively and negatively. This is highly regulated by the lymphoid cells (suggested above as self/not-self determinants) as well as by external influences from the brain or the endocrine glands. A new population of lymphoid cells, the natural killer cells, circulate in blood, lymph nodes, spleen and other lymphoid tissues and attack tumour cells, virus-infected cells and embryonic cells which are out of place.

In the immunological abnormality of AIDS patients, the absolute numbers of lymphocytes are low; T-4 (helper cells) are 10; and T-5,4 (helper/inducer cells) are both low and inverted in ratio (Good, 1984). It is not clear what happens to the natural killer cells, as amounts present in AIDS victims vary enormously. The interaction of lymphoid cells is extremely disturbed in AIDS patients; medicine refers to this as the depression of autologous mixed lymphocyte reaction and allogenic and mixed lymphocyte reaction. There are also B-cell disturbances, resulting in a near chaos of unresolved scientific problems. I have presented just a few of the facts about AIDS to the lay reader in an attempt to show the complexity and confusion within the immune system in this disease.

In view of this complicated and dangerous set of cross-triggers and unknown response confusion in the immune system, the World Health Organization (WHO Workshop, 1987) has proposed that an AIDS vaccine would need long-term B-cell memory and memory for T-helper cells and cytotoxic cells. T-lymphocytes do not usually require viral antigenic determinants for the induction of neutralizing antibodies; however, as mentioned above, the virus-infected cells are susceptible to lysis with natural killer cells. This has created an insurmountable problem for the immune system so far.

References

Acheson, E. D. and Truelove, S. C. 1961. Early weaning in the aetiology of ulcerative colitis. *British Medical Journal* 2: 929–33.

Addington-Symonds, John. 1897. A problem in Greek ethics. Repr. in *Studies in the Psychology of Sex.* Ed. H. Ellis. Vol. 1, appendix A. New York: 1975.

Alkins, H. and Newman, A. 1978. *Beecham Stories.* London: Robson Books.

Aristophanes of Byzantium, ed. 1885. Excertorum Constantini: De natural animalium libre duo. *Supplementum Aristotelicam* 1:1. Berlin.

Aristotle. 1926. *Nicomachean Ethics.* Trans. H. Rackham. New York.

Atwood, M. A. 1960. *Hermetic Philosophy and Alchemy.* New York: Julian Press.

Balint, M. 1965. Perversions and genitality. *Perversions, Psychodynamics and Therapy.* London.

Beebe, J. 1990. Toward an image of male partnership. *Psychological Perspectives* 23: 111.

———, ed. 1989. *C. G. Jung: Aspects of the Masculine.* London: Ark Paperbacks.

Boethius. n.d. Liber de persona et duabis naturis. *Patrologiae cursus completus* 64: 1341–2.

Boswell, J. 1977. *The Royal Treasure: Muslim Communities Under the Crown of Aragon in the Fourteenth Century.* New Haven.

———. 1980. *Christianity, Social Tolerance and Homosexuality.* Chicago and London: University of Chicago Press.

Brehier, E. 1965. *The History of Philosophy: The Hellenic Age.* Chicago: University of Chicago Press.

Bulletin of the World Health Organization. 1987. Immunological aspects of the prevention of viral dise~se. WHO Workshop. 65: 1–11.

Burch, P. R. J. and Burwell, L. G. 1965. Seif and not-self. *Quarterly Review of Biology* 40: 3–21.

Burnet, J. 1962. *Early Greek Philosophy.* Cleveland: Meridian.

Burnett, M. 1962. *The Integrity of the Body.* Oxford: Oxford University Press.

Centeres, R. 1972. The completion hypothesis and the compensatory dynamic in intersexual attraction and love. *Journal of Psychology* 82: 117–26.

Costello, J. 1994. Personal communication.

Danielou, A. 1964. *Hindu Polytheism.* New York: Pantheon.

Devereux, G. 1936. Sexual life of the Mohave Indians. Dissertation. University of California.

Duvall, E. M. and Duvall, S. M. 1961. *Sex Ways in Fact and Faith.* New York: Association Press.

Edinger, E. 1978. Psychology and alchemy. *Quadrant* 11.1: 12–16.

———. 1978. Solutio. *Quadrant* 11.2: 2.

———. 1979. Coagulatio. *Quadrant* 12.1: 27.

———. 1980. Sublimatio. *Quadrant* 13.1: 72.

Eriugena [or Johannis Scotti], ed. 1968. Eriugenui Periphyseon (Le divisione naturae) Scriptores. Ed. I. P. Sheldon-Williams. Dublin. *Latini Hiberniae* 7.

Fenichel, O. 1945. *The Psychoanalytic Theory of Neurosis.* New York.

Figlio, K. 1985. Personal communication.

Fisher, C., Gross, J., and Zuch, J. 1956. Cycle of penile erection synchronous with dreaming (REM) sleep. *Archives of General Psychiatry* 12: 29–45.

Fordham, M. 1957. *New Developments in Analytical Psychology.* London: Routledge and Kegan Paul.

Freud, S. 1914. On narcissism: an introduction. Standard Edition 14: 67. London: Hogarth Press and the Institute of Psychoanalysis.

Gebhard, P. et al. 1965. *Sex Offenders.* New York: Harper & Row.

Gell, P. G. H. 1957. On the nature of some hypersensitivity reactions. Ed. B. M. Halpern. *Psychopathology of the Reticulo-Endothelial System.* Oxford: Blackwell.

Gibbon, E. 1898. *The History of the Decline and Fall of the Roman Empire.* London.

Goethe, J. W. von. 1963. *Goethes Werke.* Vol. 12. Hamburg.

Good, R. A. 1984. Immunologic aberrations: the AIDS defect. Ed. K. M. Kahill. *The AIDS Epidemic.* London: Hutchinson.

Hannah, B. 1981. *Active Imagination.* Boston: Sigo Press.

Heidenstram, O., ed. 1976. *Man's Body.* London: Paddington Press.

Hillman, J. 1966. The masturbation inhibition. *Journal of Analytical Psychology* 11.1: 49–62.

Hillman, J. and von Franz, M. 1971. *Lectures on Jung's Typology.* New York: Spring Publications.

Hopcke, R. H. 1989. *Jung, Jungians and Homosexuality.* Boston and London: Shambhala.

Hoskisson, J. B. 1963. *Loneliness: An Explanation, a Cure.* London: Thorsons.

Jacoby, M. 1994. *Shame and the Origins of Self-Esteem.* New York & London: Routledge.

Jung, C. G. 1909. The significance of the father in the destiny of the individual. In *CW* 4: 301–23. London: Routledge & Kegan Paul, 1961.

———. 1921. Definitions. In *CW* 6: 408–86. London: Routledge & Kegan Paul, 1971.

———. 1937. Psychological factors in human behavior. In *CW* 8: 114–26. London: Routledge & Kegan Paul, 1960.

———. 1940. The psychology of the child archetype. In *CW* 9.1. London: Routledge & Kegan Paul, 1959.

———. 1941. Paracelsus as a spiritual phenomenon. In *CW* 13: 109–90. London: Routledge & Kegan Paul, 1967.

———. 1944. The psychic nature of the alchemical work. In *CW* 12: 242–87. London: Routledge & Kegan Paul, 1953.

———. 1945. The phenomenology of the spirit in fairy tales. In *CW* 9.1: 207–54. London: Routledge & Kegan Paul, 1959.

———. 1950. The syzygy, anima and animus. In *CW* 9.2: 11–22. London: Routledge & Kegan Paul, 1959.

_____. 1952. The battle for deliverance from the mother. In *CW* 5: 274–305. London: Routledge & Kegan Paul, 1956.

_____. 1961. *Memories, Dreams, Reflections*. New York: Vintage.

_____. 1971. *Psychological Types. CW* 6. London: Routledge & Kegan Paul.

Kast, V. 1991. *Sisyphus: A Jungian Approach to Midlife Crisis*. Einsiedeln: Daimon Verlag.

Kay, D. 1985. Paternal psychopathology and the emerging ego. *The Father*. Ed. A. Samuels. London: Free Association Books. 45–68.

Kelly, E. 1893. *The Alchemical Writings of Edward Kelly*. London: J. Elliot and Co.

Kernberg, O. 1975. *Borderline Conditions and Pathological Narcissism*. New York.

Kinsey, A. 1941. Homosexuality: a criterion for a hormonal explanation of the homosexual. *Journal of Clinical Endocrinology* 1.5: 424–28.

_____. 1948. *Sexual Behavior in the Human Male*. Philadelphia: W. B. Saunders.

_____. 1951. The causes of homosexuality: a symposium. *Sexology* 21.9: 558–62.

Kinsey, A. C., et al. 1948. *Sexual Behavior in the Human Male*. Philadelphia: Saunders.

Kohut, H. 1970. The Self: a contribution to its place in theory and technique. *International Journal of Psycho-Analysis* 51: 176.

Lacan, J. 1949. 1977. The mirror stage as formative of the function of the I as revealed in psychoanalytic experience. *Ecrits*. Trans. A. Sheridan. London: Tavistock.

Layland, W. R. 1981. In search of a loving father. *International Journal of Psycho-Analysis* 62.2: 2156224.

Libby, F. 1965. Make place in the physical universe. Ed. J. R. Platt. *New Views on the Nature of Man*. Chicago: University of Chicago Press.

Lopez-Pedraza, R. 1976. The tale of Dryops and the birth of Pan. *Spring*.

_____. 1977. *Hermes and His Children*. Zurich: Spring Publications.

Lu K'uan Yu. 1970. *Taoist Yoga: Alchemy and Immortality*. London: Rider.

Mahler, M. 1971. A study of separation-individuation process. *Psycho-Analytical Study of the Child* 26:403–24. London: New Quadrangle.

Maimonides, M. The Book of Holiness. Book 5. *The Code of Maimonides*. Trans. L. Rabinowitz and P. Grossman. *Yale Judaica Series* 16. New York.

Masters, W. H. and Johnson, V. E. 1979. *Homosexuality in Perspective*. Boston: Little, Brown.

McDougall, J. 1972. Primal scene and sexual perversion. *International Journal of Psycho-Analysis* 53: 371.

Medawar, P. B. 1957. *The Uniqueness of the Individual*. London: Methuen.

Michael, R. P. and Zumpe, D. 1979. Biological factors in the organization and expression of sexual behavior. Ed. I. Rosen. *Sexual Deviation*. Oxford: Oxford University Press.

Monick, E. 1987. *Phallos: Sacred Image of the Masculine*. Toronto: Inner City Books.

Neumann, E. 1959. The significance of the genetic aspect for analytical psychology. *Journal of Analytical Psychology* 4: 125–38.

Otto, W. 1979. *The Homeric Gods*. London: Thames and Hudson.

Parrish, W. E. 1966. Antibody to sperm. *International Medical Tribunal of Great Britain* 1: 29–41.

Plato. 1932. *Symposium*. 2nd ed. Trans. R. G. Bury. Loeb Classical Library ed. Cambridge, MA: Heinemann & Harvard University Press. 182b-D.

Plutarch. *Moralia*. Trans. W. C. Helmhold. *Dialogue on Love*. London. 767.

Read, J., ed. 1963. *Prelude to Chemistry: An Outline of Alchemy*. London: Stuart.

Reich, A. 1951. The discussion of 1912 on masturbation and our present-day views. *Psycho-Analytical Study of the Child* 6: 80–94.

Reinisch, J. M. and Beasley, R. 1991. *The Kinsey Institute New Report on Sex*. London: Penguin.

Rosen, I. 1979. Perversion as a regulator of self-esteem. *Sexual Deviation*. Oxford: Oxford University Press.

Ryce-Menuhin, J. 1988. *The Self in Early Childhood*. London: Free Association Books.

Samuels, A. ed. 1985. *The Father: Contemporary Jungian Perspectives*. London: Free Association Books.

———. 1976. *The Plural Psyche: Personality, Morality and the Father*. London and New York: Routledge.

Samuels, A., Shorter, B., and Plaut, F. 1986. *A Critical Dictionary of Jungian Analysis*. London: Routledge and Kegan Paul.

Singer, J. 1976. *Androgyny: Towards a New Theory of Sexuality*. Garden City, New Jersey: Doubleday.

Spitz, R. A. Auto-erotism re-examined. *Psycho-Analytical Study of the Child* 17: 283–315.

Stein, L. 1967. Introducing not-self. *Journal of Analytical Psychology* 12: 97–114.

Stein, M. 1983. *In Midlife: A Jungian Perspective*. Dallas: Spring Publications.

Stekel, W. 1951. *Auto-Erotism: A Psychiatric Study of Masturbation and Neurosis*. London: Nevill.

Stevens, A. 1982. *Archetypes: A Natural History of the Self*. New York and London: Routledge.

———. 1990. *On Jung*. New York and London: Routledge.

Turnbull, L. and Hawk, R. 1966. *World Medicine* 19 July: 23.

Village Voice. 1975. Quoted from Wilson, G. and Niss, D. 1977. *Love's Mysteries*. New York: Fontana. 32–3.

Waite, E. A., trans. 1953. Hermetic Museum I:40. London: Watkins.

———. 1969. *The Hermetic and Alchemical Writings of Paracelsus*. New Hyde Park, New York: Universal Books Incorporates 1: 4.

Walsh, D. 1978. Homosexuality, rationality and Western culture. *Harvest* 24.

Wiggens, J. S., Wiggens, N., and Conger, J. A. 1968. Correlates of heterosexual somatic preference. *Journal of Personality and Social Psychology* 10: 82–90.

Winnicott, D. 1967. Mirror role of mother and family in child development. *Playing and Reality*. London: Tavistock, 1971.

Zimmer, H. 1952. *Philosophies of India*. New York: Pantheon.

Index